What Re

"This is an excellent book that every stepmom should own. This is not the kind of book you pick up and read in one day — this is the kind of book where you read one topic, you pray, and you pause and take in what you just read. It's a book that you carry with you throughout the day in your heart."

~~ Janet Heberling
Blended Family Ministry Leader,
Christ Church at Grove Farm, Pennsylvania

"Karon Goodman writes an outstanding book that will inspire everyone and give all who read it a deeper sense that God is the anchor when life's storms hit. It's a stepmom's guide to comfort through scripture, a book to be read over and over."

~~ Christy Borgeld
Founder, Stepfamily Day

A Stepmom's Book of Prayer

Seeking God, Growing Strong, Finding Peace

Karon Phillips Goodman

More Books from Karon

The Stepmom's Guide to Simplifying Your Life

It's Not My Stepkids — It's Their Mom!

You're Late Again, Lord!
The Impatient Woman's Guide to God's Timing

Grab a Broom, Lord — There's Dust Everywhere!
The Imperfect Woman's Guide to God's Grace

You Still Here, Lord?
The Insecure Woman's Guide to God's Faithfulness

Everyday Angels
Simple Ways to Be an Angel Everyday

http://KaronGoodman.com

Dedication

*To all the stepmoms everywhere
who need our prayers. May we
support and sustain one another
in God's love and care.*

Acknowledgements

I'm so honored to have been touched by the lives of the many stepmoms who inspired and continue to support this book. The sisterhood of stepmoms who understand each other without a word is an amazingly strong and powerful group. They are truly the Lord's disciples in unlikely gear.

I want to thank Marnie Pehrson who held my hand through our publication process. I'm grateful for her kindness and abilities and complete control of the situation when I had none! I greatly appreciate all of those who gave a part of themselves for this book, including my husband and my boys, even though they'll probably never realize the wonderful gifts they've given me. And I'm truly honored to have Nicole's Foreword and the stories from Paige, Shauna, Sue, Kimberly and Liza to include for you here.

Finally, I thank *you*, my reader, for joining me on this journey of prayer. Thank you for opening yourself up to the grace of God and reaching out to those around you to share it.

Contents

Foreword

It's quiet. It's early. My coffee is hot. The sky is still black. The world is still asleep. The day is coming.

In a few moments the day will arrive. It will roar down the track with the rising of the sun. The stillness of the dawn will be exchanged for the noise of the day. The calm of the solitude will be replaced by the pounding pace of the human race. The refuge of the early morning will be invaded by decisions to be made and deadlines to be met. For the next twelve hours I will be exposed to the day's demands.

It is now that I should pray for strength…but there is so much to do. Before I know it, my mind is caught up in the details of the day…emails to attend to, deadlines to chart, checkups to schedule, grocery lists to make, breakfast to cook and bottles to make. Already, my mind is so far away from Him that I can't possibly find the peace He has planned for me.

As I stumble through my tasks, my conscience starts to get to me. When I remember how Jesus taught us to pray, it's so evident to me that He doesn't necessarily want us to repeat the words. He wants us to grasp the message of loving, living, breathing communication in His example:

"9 Pray then like this: Our Father who art in heaven, Hallowed be thy name. 10 Thy kingdom come. Thy will be done, On earth as it is in heaven. 11 Give us this day our daily bread; 12 And forgive us our debts, As we also have forgiven our debtors; 13 And lead us not into temptation, But deliver us from evil." ~ Matthew 6:9-13 {RSV}

"Our Father, who art in Heaven, Hallowed be thy name."   What a poetic way to remind us that our Father, our intimate and loving Father, is in control! What problems could I possibly have that can't be handled by my Father, who is in Heaven, whose name is honored and praised by all creation?

"Your Kingdom come," There is no other who can compare to our Heavenly Father. He reminds us that we are on a journey, and our ultimate reward lies in the fact that God does rule over all and His Kingdom will reign over every trial and hurdle we must face.

"Thy will be done on Earth as it is in Heaven," Praying for God's will is a beautiful reminder that God only desires to give us the very best. We shouldn't come to the Father with a shopping list. We should come humbly, seeking His face and His good will in our lives, because like any loving Father — He wants the best for His children.

"Give us this day our daily bread,"   We fool ourselves if we think we have anything beautiful and good in our lives as a result of our own strengths and talents. Our talents are gifts God has given us to make our way in this world. The opportunities for knowledge and skill are also from God. In His Mercy and Grace, He gave them to us. Our needs (not necessarily our wants) will always be taken care of if we simply hand the task over to our loving, caring Father.

"Forgive us our debts as we forgive our debtors," It is no accident that Jesus included this part in His example of prayer. We should forgive those who caused us pain. We are forgiven of our sins to the

same degree that we forgive others. Jesus shows us to release the judgment to God the Father and not seek our own revenge. Harboring resentments and revenge creates a self-made prison by our own choosing. Our Father is a God of reconciliation. He set the example with Jesus who paid the price to set us free. He knew that by releasing those who have sinned against us, that we would live a life blessed and filled with joy and happiness...a life ready to receive His blessings. It's impossible to live in peace when barriers of resentment and revenge stand in our way.

"Lead us not into temptation, but deliver us from evil." If we were never tempted, we would never understand or know the will of God and His power to keep us from all forms of evil. We are only a prayer away — and He wants us to pray to help us overcome temptation and grow in faith and character as a Christian. God has promised that He won't allow us to be tempted beyond what we can bear. (*See I Corinthians 10:13*) Praying for His help in our daily trials is a loving reminder that nothing is too difficult for Him to guide us through.

God has shown Himself to have a very unique way of speaking to us in our daily lives...burning bushes, apparitions, angels. God does speak to us, and the list of His vessels goes on. Remaining in a state of constant prayer enables our hearts to stay open to Him, so He can speak through even the simplest of means...even through our "still, small voice."

So I stop and pray. *"Father God, thank You for Your Holiness and Your Power over my life, and thank You for calling me back to You through Your Truth this morning. I pray for Your loving will to be done in my life today. Use me as a vessel to speak Your Truth and continue Your loving care of my family and me as I follow the path You have set before me. Forgive me, Lord, for my sins and my shortcomings. Help me, Lord, to forgive those who let me down, as well. Please help me to remember that the journey is mine, and the judgment is Yours. Help me to remember Your example of love in all of my encounters today. Help me, Lord, to claim Your victory over the temptations I will face today, and help me to be a loving example of Your kindness in all of my exchanges. Thank You for You, and for the me I am striving to be. Amen."*

The sun is rising now. My coffee's gone. The birds are singing in the new day. My chaos is gone, and I face today with a smile of peace. God did it again. He conquered my noise with His song.

The path of stepparenting isn't always an easy one. Thankfully, for us, God knows our journey, and He knows our trials. He knows our needs before we even speak them. Finding peace in that Power is only a prayer away....

Nicole L. Weyant, Certified Blended Family Consultant and founder of the online blended family support group, *iStepfamily.com* {www.istepfamily.com}. She is an active member of the American Association of Christian Counselors and the International Association of Coaches. Nicole maintains an online practice at *The Blended Family Life Center* {www.blendedfamilylifecenter.com}.

Introduction

Praying anyway, the only way...

But I call to God, and the Lord saves me.
Evening, morning and noon I cry out in distress,
and he hears my voice.
Psalm 55:16-17 {NIV}

Stepmothering is the ultimate learning experience, full of insights and discoveries, pain and joy. The role is always surprising and often exasperating. The realization of all you've gotten yourself into is sometimes overwhelming. The most important thing a stepmom learns is the most basic and sometimes the hardest to admit: *I can't do this alone.*

No one ever enters a remarriage with *little plans.* That would be too easy! We always have big ideals and bigger expectations. The world we never knew we'd live gets in the way, though, and almost everyone, including us, will fall short of those expectations. Very little happens the way we envision, and we often deal with thoughts and emotions and fears that shock and consume us.

The faith we claimed and felt before we became stepmoms is tested. Sometimes it's broken. The past depresses us, the present exhausts us, and the future terrifies us. We're tempted to give up, to let the pain win, to abandon our hopes for happiness. Sadly, many stepmoms do.

As many as two-thirds of all remarriages with children involved end, often before the fourth anniversary. Before I became a stepmom, that statistic would probably have surprised me, because you think that people who remarry must be truly happy, so thankful to have been given a second chance at the kind of love everybody wants. How could those couples ever fail?

Then when I became a stepmom and walked through my own hell, I was surprised that the percentage was only two-thirds. I'll bet that all of us have wondered — maybe even just once in the most private of moments — if we could make it, if we would ever get through the pain and confusion that threatened our marriages, and even more, our faith. That's when it's time to stop questioning your faith and start relying on it instead. That's when you cry out, "Help me!" and the Lord responds.

> *For I, the Lord your God, will hold your right hand,*
> *Saying to you, 'Fear not, I will help you.'*
> Isaiah 41:13 {NKJV}

In this book, we'll go through four stages of a stepmom's life and faith: *Beginning, Struggling, Coping* and *Growing*. While we're all different, we are all very much the same: helping to raise another woman's children, trying to keep a burdened marriage together, having to learn when we fit in our unexpected lives. May these prayers help and comfort you and bring you joy and peace.

Stop. Pray. Go.

A Stepmom Prays . . .

One day in prayer, I questioned God as to His knowledge of a blended family. Can you imagine questioning God's knowledge? It sounds so disrespectful, but God has a way of extending His grace abundantly to our lives over and over again.

I had been feeling defeated as a "step" mother to my new children. God's word always had the answer to my questions, but I could not find the answer to this one.

I sat quietly, listening for that voice that comes from deep within your soul and ministers to your heart. Then I heard, *"My Son was a stepchild, and part of a blended family."*

That statement startled me. I reread the story in Matthew, chapter 1, of Jesus' conception, Joseph and Mary's quiet marriage, and Jesus' birth. How many times I had read this passage, yet never seen that Joseph was Jesus' stepfather. What an awesome task God had given to Joseph, a simple carpenter — to raise the Son of God. The very breath of God was in their family! He was giving me an awesome task, too.

My prayer: God, breathe the breath of Your spirit into my life and family. Joseph learned through his humility that he could become an excellent father to Your Son. I want to be an excellent mother to these children that You have put into my life. You know me better than I know myself, yet You trust me, in all my weaknesses, with these precious lives. I sit at Your cross, waiting and listening for Your instruction. Teach me Your ways. Amen.

~~ **Paige Becnel**, *mother of two, stepmother of three,* Associate Pastor, Healing Place Church Author: *"God Breathes on Blended Families"*

Beginning

When you pass through the waters, I will be with you;
And through the rivers, they shall not overflow you.
When you walk through the fire, you shall not be burned,
Nor shall the flame scorch you.
For I am the Lord your God.
Isaiah 43:2-3 {NKJV}

The stepmom sat in the dark in her living room floor, crying again, still. She prayed a non-sensical prayer, needing everything, understanding nothing. She felt lost and alone, afraid and defeated. She was watching her world collapse around her, the new world she had tried so hard to create and protect.

That stepmom was me. Maybe it's you, too. It was a long while ago that I felt so hopeless, but the feelings are easily beckoned to the surface. *It should be easier*, I kept telling myself. *Why is this so hard?*

When I could calm down and string two thoughts together, I could find lots of answers to that question — my husband, his kids, mine, their other parents, time, money, jealousy, insecurity deeper than space — every thing that touched me each day. My life was so hard because it was the life of a stepmom, a bewildered creature afraid and unprepared for a most treacherous journey.

Understanding the causes of my sadness was helpful, and finding ways to deal with the pain mandatory. But there was one step that had to come first, and it was a surprisingly hard stretch of faith, because I thought it meant admitting more failure.

Instead, it meant finding the only beginning to a better life. I had to stop trying to carry the burden of my stepmotherhood by myself. I had to rediscover God's strength, courage and peace, go to the safest place that was waiting for me. I had to open my eyes and my heart to a power much bigger than I am, ask for guidance and let God provide it.

Stop. Pray. Go.

Often, I couldn't even form the words to turn my fears and hurts into a logical prayer. God didn't mind. He knew my pain as well as I did. He was there to help. He always is.

* * * * *

Beginning (or Beginning Again) in the Life of a Stepmom

Love
Fear
Doubt
Insecurity
Patience

A Stepmom's Prayer of Love

Love is patient, love is kind. It does not envy,
it does not boast, it is not proud. It is not rude, it is not
self-seeking, it is not easily angered, it keeps no record of
wrongs. Love does not delight in evil but rejoices with the
truth. It always protects, always trusts, always hopes,
always perseveres.
1 Corinthians 13:4-7 {NIV}

Love truly is blind. It hides the obvious and obscures the dangers. It makes us throw more than caution to the wind. We may throw reason, fear, hurt and anger away while we feast on the undeniable emotion that consumes us like no other. Especially if you've experienced a loveless or neglectful marriage, the love that envelopes you with your new husband feels strong enough to banish even the biggest stepfamily worries. Love is blind to all that would threaten it, and so are we. At least for a while.

Sooner or later, the reality of a family before this one hits, and it brings all kinds of problems with it. The daily burdens can outweigh the amazing love we thought we had. When we have to look at those outside forces that become more real every day, we sometimes retreat, afraid that what we've trusted isn't there any more, afraid that what's *opposing* us is stronger than what's *supporting* us. Has the love you felt mutinied you to stand alone to fight for your life?

It can feel like it sometimes. As the challenges of your life become more visible and more difficult, your stress increases and it becomes hard to recall the warm and nurturing thoughts and feelings you felt for your husband even a short while ago, or to remember what it felt like to receive those from him.

We can become so burdened, afraid, angry and overwhelmed that we have more feelings of resentment than love. But the love hasn't changed — it's just masked by the problems that hurt so much. It's not been defeated; it's just waiting for you to put it into battle.

One against the world

Find comfort in the safety of the love that you and your husband feel for each other, and work to unleash it when the world gets you down. Fight your way through your struggles with a constant grip on the force that brought you two together in the first place. Do what you must to protect and reclaim your love of a lifetime. And then let *your love* protect *you*.

It's you and your husband as one against the world. Your love isn't a fairy tale; it's a living, breathing extension of God's love that will sustain you when you're weak. It's strong when you *believe* it is and work to make it even stronger by giving it the chance to shine. Ask the Lord to show you ways to express your love, to accept more love, and to let your love work in all aspects of your life.

Love at work

When your heart is hurting or your mind is full of worry and you can't think any more, take all of those thoughts and mentally throw them on the floor. Replace each one with a single happy memory that washes the love you and your husband have all over you like sunshine. Breathe in and feel that love energizing you. Then you can rest for a while and have the strength to think again. It sounds too simple, but it's a strong place to start.

Every happy moment, every tiny action that epitomizes the love you two share — give thanks for them all. Thank God for the true and honest love that you've been blessed with, and honor it each day by never taking it for granted. You and your husband can use your love to navigate the jagged shoreline of your lives. And it's powerful enough to guide you each step of the way.

Protective love

Love is uniquely qualified to protect you as you begin your steplife, or just try to make it better. Because your love has grown from loss and grief and often in a hostile environment, you will be extremely reluctant to give it up. The more you revere and celebrate that love, the more it insulates you from the pitfalls of your life.

If your stepkids' mom attacks you, you have a shield to stand between you and her, a love that isn't afraid and isn't weak. If your stepkids are difficult, you have a foundation that keeps you going when the going feels impossible.

The love you have is strong and meant to be *used*. Call on it and let it do its job.

Nurtured love

Even when you're fending off attacks or fighting battles anew, remember that your love is something to be cherished. It is a true gift, and you increase its value with attention and devotion.

In all of the turmoil going on around you, remember to put nurturing your love at the top of your list. You spend time with God every day because you love Him and need Him. Do the same with your husband, regardless of what else is happening. See that love exemplified is a constant in your lives. None of us can keep up with this job without a daily shower of love! *Let all that you do be done with love* {1 Corinthians 16:14 NKJV}.

Love reflected

We know how much we need God's love to handle the role of stepmom. And strangely enough, we get even more when we give it away. Like the loaves and fishes, the more we act and react out of love, the more love the Lord pours into our lives.

Sometimes, it's hard to see that, isn't it?! That doesn't matter, though, because we learn to see with our heart, to feel *inside* the conviction of a love-filled life. Don't be afraid to give out more love than you expect to receive. It's not a competition. It is a chosen way to live your life, and adding the role of stepmom just expands it a little.

Nothing changes about God's love, and He always fills us with more than enough to do our job and meet every responsibility we have. You can trust Him in that.

> *The only thing that counts is faith*
> *expressing itself through love.*
> Galatians 5:6 {NIV}

To Think About: What makes you feel loved by your husband? Tell him about it. In what ways do you show your husband that you love him every day? How can you let your love protect you more in your struggles? What role does God's love play in your life and role as stepmom? How can you reflect His love every day?

To God in Prayer: *Lord, thank You for the love that my husband and I feel for each other. We are on a difficult mission, we recognize the challenges, and we need You in every way. Please help us to always value our love and to use its power to protect and sustain us. Help us to spread that love to our children and to build upon it a safe and secure home for us all. Amen.*

A Stepmom's Prayer
for Overcoming Fear

For God has not given us a spirit of fear,
but of power and of love and of a sound mind.
2 Timothy 1:7 {NKJV}

Regardless of how much you prepare for your stepfamily, there is no way to predict the deep fear that can overtake you. It's easy to become afraid of everything, especially failing in this marriage you've worked so hard to have. Or you might be afraid of being rejected by your stepkids, or that you'll never love or like them. Maybe you're afraid you've made a mistake, that you won't be able to handle the problems and complications of a burdened marriage and kids you didn't give birth to. What do you do with that paralyzing kind of fear? There's only one effective response to the fear, and it's a faith undaunted.

We sometimes let our fears get bigger than they have to be. We generalize and sensationalize and dramatize until we can't see around our fears enough to deal with them. They grab us by the heart and keep us from finding any happiness and peace. Even the good moments are barely enjoyed when the fears are so strong. But there is something stronger that's both practical and spiritual. And it's essential for stepmoms.

A faith strong enough

Faith is the only thing big enough to counteract the fear. But it's not a vague or far away faith. It's one that you can hold onto today, right now, because it's *inside* you. It's a faith from a God Who will never let you down — a deep belief that you will find a way to cope with everything and survive what's happening to you when you go to Him in complete confidence that He will respond to your pain.

He got up, rebuked the wind and said to the waves,
"Quiet! Be still!" Then the wind died down and it was
completely calm. He said to his disciples, "Why are
you so afraid? Do you still have no faith?"
Mark 4:39-40 {NIV}

He can quiet the waves in your life, too, those now and those to come. No, you don't know everything that will happen with your family. You don't know how your marriage will be tested or how your relationship with your stepchildren will grow, but that's okay. You can face all of that without fear if you choose to go on, to put one foot in front of the other, one day at a time, and if you have faith in God to help you through. He never said this would be easy, but He did say that He would never abandon you in this or any other difficulty.

I sought the Lord, and He heard me,
And delivered me from all my fears.
Psalm 34:4 {NKJV}

Trust that God will help you through whatever happens, and then put your energies into finding better approaches and solutions instead of worrying about failing. You'll be able to handle whatever happens if you talk to God first — and have faith that He will hear you.

Practical faith

If instead, you let the fear set up shop in your heart, then you can't do the things that will help you see how powerless the fear really is. That's the practical part. With just a little faith, you can make a choice that pushes away a fear. When you look at a problem as just an obstacle and not an insurmountable issue, you can find a solution. When you see the problem or fear as just one bump in your family's road, then you can see beyond it.

That takes faith, but don't you see? It's the *practical* faith that says, "Okay, trust in yourself, your husband and your God. Pray for guidance, listen and do one thing today to help yourself get over the fear, and rejoice in what you've learned."

Fight the fear each day so that you don't let it get bigger than you are. By taking an active, practical step in the direction *opposite* your fear, you move a step closer to God. If your fear says you're going to be unloved by your stepkids, your faith says follow God's guidance and love them first. Do whatever is more about Him and less about the fear. And He won't leave you alone.

Spirited faith

Of course, you've heard that most of the things we fear never come to pass anyway. That's little comfort if you're living a threatened marriage or a stepmom/stepchild relationship that seems to thrive on hate. Then it's hard to just dismiss that fear with a seemingly nonchalant thought. But *spirited* faith is more than that.

Having faith in God's ability to handle
everything and trusting Him to help *you* handle
everything makes taking those practical steps easier.
You can meet and defeat your fears with a sincere act
of faith. You don't have to just *will* the fears away —
you can take steps each day to *send* them away,
leaning on a God who is stronger than anything this
life brings. There is no problem bigger than He is.

> *There is no fear in love;*
> *but perfect love casts out fear.*
> 1 John 4:18 {NKJV}

For example, set aside a time to talk to your
husband and explain to him what's scaring you,
come up with a plan together, and reinforce your
commitment to each other. Then the fear is pushed to
the back of your mind and a calming faith in the life
you've chosen takes center stage. And your marriage
is stronger, too. That tiny tiptoe of faith builds on
itself and soon, the fear can't get a decent footing.
Soon, you've defeated the fear that threatened your
peace.

Steady faith

If you're afraid that you'll never have the
relationship you want with your stepkids, realize
that your faith can outlast the fear if you let it. Walk
slowly in faith to work in even the tiniest ways to
build that relationship you want. Take one crisis at a
time, implementing one practical idea at a time,
responding to your stepchild's actions one response
at a time. Build on what's good and reject what's
bad. Have faith that you will build as much as your

stepchild will let you because you can choose to build while you wait — not fear that you won't.

You don't have to fear something that can always improve over time. If you are too afraid to move, you'll miss the opportunities that do present themselves and overlook the slightest bit of progress. Your fears about stepmotherhood are groundless when countered with a true and steady faith in your God. He knows, though, how scared we get and how lost we feel. That's why He's never farther away than a prayer, why He's always exactly what we need.

The Lord is my light and my salvation;
Whom shall I fear? The Lord is the strength
of my life; Of whom shall I be afraid?
Psalm 27:1 {NKJV}

To Think About: What are your biggest fears? How much of your life have they already consumed? What practical steps can you take today to overcome them? How can you reinforce and call upon your faith to get you through your fears?

To God in Prayer: *Lord, You know these fears that paralyze me sometimes. I need to take care of myself and my family and not be afraid of that which I cannot control. Please help me to replace worry with action, listen to Your guidance, and find a way to banish these fears that are standing in the way of my happiness. I don't want to be afraid anymore. Amen.*

A Stepmom's Prayer for Overcoming Doubt

If any of you lacks wisdom, he should ask God, who gives generously to all without finding fault, and it will be given to him. But when he asks, he must believe and not doubt, because he who doubts is like a wave of the sea, blown and tossed by the wind.
James 1:5-6 {NIV}

Few things can destroy your confidence and make you question your future like becoming a stepmom. Every day brings a new problem that you never thought you'd be thinking about. How could you have prepared, and now, how can you respond to everything that's going on around you? When you need a strong heart and belief in your abilities, that's exactly when you can't feel it. And where is God to help you with all this? How can you deal with the doubt that's overtaking your every thought?

You may have been surprised at how quickly your confidence has eroded — in everything. And it's particularly unsettling when you begin to doubt God, when you feel so lost and alone that you wonder if perhaps you've been abandoned. Where is the help and comfort that you're needing now?

And where is the hope and promise that you began this life with? Your faith in your husband may be tested, your patience with your stepkids may vanish, and your decision to marry may look like less than a great idea. The troubling doubts that creep into every thought can derail you quickly from your path. Knowing where the doubts come from is part of the answer. Choosing to defeat them is the other part.

Doubts understood

Whether the doubts are about your feelings for your life now, your abilities, or your worries about God's presence in your life, the answer is the same: restore your confidence and the doubts go away. Restoring your confidence won't be quick, but you can take it one step at a time and build on your successes. Every time you replace a doubt with a truth, you push every other doubt farther away.

Let's look at your doubts about your feelings first. It's easy to be overwhelmed with anger, worry and sadness — even to the point of feeling only those negative emotions and not feeling any positive ones. That's when you can start doubting the very basis of your life now, your love and devotion to your husband. If you're not careful, the anger, worry and sadness will win. You have to have something stronger to beat them.

Go to the source of your pain and see if you can identify exactly what is creating the doubt in your mind. Is it a nagging feeling you have, a single episode that's bothering you? Has someone said or done something to make you question your own feelings? Look deep into your doubt. Write down in one sentence what it is and why you feel that way, maybe: *I wonder if I've made a mistake with this marriage because I've given up so much and receive so little in return.*

Doubts defeated

Then you can choose to defeat that doubt with a truth — you respond with a force that can beat it. You find something just as powerful right away and do it: Have some alone time with your husband, write about an especially comforting time, plan a family outing, take a break so that you can recharge and get a better perspective on things — anything positive that reconnects you with your true heart. Resolve to put your doubt away for at least 24 hours and look for only reaffirming truths during that time. I know that you can find at least one truth that will give a boost to your confidence in yourself and your choices.

Do you doubt your ability to handle the life of a stepmom? Please don't. You can manage this role just like you do all your other roles: with God's help and a clear plan. Again, write down your doubts most prevalent. Maybe it's a doubt that you'll ever love your stepchildren, that they'll ever accept you, that you'll ever bond with them given their mom's opinion of you. All of that baggage is real, but it's not more powerful than your strength and will to be the stepmom you want to be.

Trust yourself to learn this role, ask God to direct you, and do one positive thing today that restores a little confidence, even if it's as simple as having a calm conversation with your stepdaughter. One step at a time is enough.

The more damaging doubt

Now let's look at your doubts about finding God in your pain. Do you feel that He's forsaken you to deal with this mess yourself? That's easy to do, especially in the raw worry of a new stepfamily. Write that down, too: *I don't know where God is now that I need Him so. Why doesn't He answer my prayers?*

Then you choose to defeat that painful doubt with a truth, too. When has He ever abandoned you? When has He not given you the wisdom or courage or strength that you needed when you asked Him sincerely? When has He ever been unfaithful to you? How strong is your side of this argument?

Now is just another part of your journey. The scenery changes, but the Guide is the same. God is there with you always, because He can't be anywhere else. Trust Him, and you learn to trust yourself even more.

> *I will say of the Lord, "He is my refuge and*
> *my fortress, my God, in whom I trust."*
> Psalm 91:2 {NIV}

To Think About: What are your most frightening doubts, about yourself, others or God? Why have you let them into your heart, and how much are they controlling your life? Ask God to help you defeat your doubts and find the truths you need to exile them from your heart and feel a renewed devotion to your family.

To God in Prayer: *Lord, please remove all of these hurtful doubts from my heart. I need to feel You close and strong, eager to help me overcome all these questions in my mind. Please speak Your timeless truths to my spirit and guide me confidently through my role as stepmom and wife. Amen.*

A Stepmom's Prayer
for Overcoming Insecurity

He will not let your foot slip —
he who watches over you will not slumber.
Psalm 121:3 {NIV}

Perhaps the feeling more widespread than any
other among stepmoms, new or otherwise, is that of
intense insecurity. Sometimes, that insecurity can
last for months or even years, depending on how
many things there are in the stepmom's life to
threaten her sense of calm and trust. If she's lucky,
she'll only have to get through the first awkward
months of a new family. But sometimes, there are
tensions and dangers that make settling in a very
slow process.

Often the insecurity is a heavy, pervasive feeling
of not knowing where you belong. If you've come
from a difficult marriage or been abandoned, you
may have a hard time trusting your new relationship,
especially when it's saddled with the added
complications of an ex-wife and children. Sometimes,
stepmoms talk about feeling "on the outside" looking
in at what is supposed to be their new life. They
speak of a bond that their husbands have with his
kids, a sacred circle that's not easily entered.

Other stepmoms feel that they compete with their
stepchildren's mom, for the kids' affection, respect,
love, everything. Often, these stepmoms are more
'mother' to their stepkids than the kids' 'real' mom,
but still, they can feel second best all the time,
wondering if they'll ever be appreciated and feel
secure in the pivotal, yet often neglected, role they
play in the family.

And perhaps one of the worst feelings of insecurity arises from sharing your life with your husband's ex-wife. You may feel that your life exists at her mercy, that she can and will control what happens to your family. That's a debilitating kind of insecurity that will destroy you from deep inside if you don't overcome it.

The Lord's security, your security

All of the logic in the world won't help defy these insecurities you feel. You can dispel them in your mind and they will still ache in your heart — until you fill it with something else. Let the security of God's love and grace into your whole soul, and rest in the safe place He always has for you.

Be merciful to me, O God, be merciful to me!
For my soul trusts in You; And in the shadow of
Your wings I will make my refuge, Until these
calamities have passed by.
Psalm 57:1 {NKJV}

The Lord's protective arms are always around you, to comfort you and help you see everything more objectively. You can trust that He will help you feel more secure every day, and there are two seemingly contradictory ways to do that: look at each threat, and look far ahead.

Looking now

Take a few moments to look at your life as you begin each day. I know that's all you do, but on this day, identify and define anything specific that you expect to threaten your insecurity today. Then, before those events even happen, counter each with a warm and safe memory that will let you take a breath and rest for a moment. Then you can prepare.

Always talk to your husband and let him reassure you, too, because it's possible that he might see some things more objectively than you do. And apply some reason to your insecurities: your world will not end even if something *does* threaten you today. You will find a way through it because you have in the past. Always take the time to look at all you've overcome and find strength in your victories. Pray for continued guidance from your Savior, and let yourself rest in the comfort of His security, the security that will never falter.

Jesus Christ is the same yesterday, today, and forever.
Hebrews 13:8 {NKJV}

If you let the general ever-growing paranoia of insecurity envelop you, it will. But it loses its punch when you dissect it. Again, just the logic of combating your insecurities won't be enough, but it's a good start. Plan exactly how you'll respond to whatever threatens you — what you'll say or the choice you'll make. You beat the insecurities by *preparing* for them. Trust God to never leave you alone to face the situations that upset you so. God's power is so much greater than anything your life can present. He'll give you each day's required amount of strength and energy, if you'll just ask.

Looking ahead

Just as important as looking at each situation that threatens you, look at your whole life and where you want to be five, ten, twenty years from now.

Getting there will take all of your best work, and you can't give your best if nagging insecurities are wearing you down. Look beyond those insecurities to a time when you have mastered them all, when you have overcome every threat to your happiness. Look for good things to happen in your life, and anticipate your happiness in a future you and God will create.

The Lord wants you to be fulfilled in your life, to be safe and secure so that you can give to others the same things: a sense of hope and faith and first-hand knowledge of victory in overcoming the odds of a challenging life. So take a moment each day to look far ahead, perhaps to a time when the kids are grown and happy and you and your husband can reap the rewards of all your hard work.

Then when you guarantee yourself the life you want in the future, you have a better attitude about the insecurities that plague you today, granting yourself the power to dislodge them. Trust in God to lead you through the difficult and scary times with strength and blessings you can't even imagine right now, and look positively to a long time from now, when you'll wonder why you ever let the insecurities you feel today bother you for one second.

A stepmom's life may never be completely free of insecurities, but it can get better every day. And consider this: many lifestyles lead to insecurities — it's all about learning to manage them and always returning to the Lord for the strength and courage and will to go on. That's security in the greatest power of all.

To Think About: What causes you the most
insecurity in your role as stepmom? Why have you
allowed these issues to take control of your heart and
paralyze your work and progress? What would give
you more security? Ask God to help you find the
security you need for your life and trust Him to walk
the path with you.

To God in Prayer: *Lord, this insecurity I feel is
killing me inside. Please help me find in You and myself
the power to carry on and overcome all the threats I fear,
real or imagined. Show me the truths and securities of my
life that I have trouble seeing. Please guide me through
today, make me stronger and more secure, and then guide
me through tomorrow. Amen.*

A Stepmom's Prayer for Patience

Wait for the Lord; be strong and
take heart and wait for the Lord.
Psalm 27:14 {NIV}

While we're losing our sanity in this new and complicated life, we're usually losing our patience, too. Our frustration grows daily when things seem to be at a standstill, no one's cooperating, the "blending" isn't happening, and getting settled into a "normal" life sounds like pure science fiction.

It's an understandable reaction: we want everything to be right and good, and we want it *now*! We want stepchildren to be accepting, ex-spouses to be stable, and our confusion and anxiety to vanish overnight.

Sadly, we can't have all of that, or at least not as quickly as we wished we could. The dynamics of a stepfamily may stretch realization of those ideals to six, eight, even ten years or more. But no matter how long it takes for us to adapt to our role, the Lord will not abandon us in our journey.

He who began a good work in you will carry it
on to completion until the day of Christ Jesus.
Philippians 1:6 {NIV}

Why patience is scarce

A new stepmom is anxious for her family to "work," to be the safe and warm place that nurtures everyone and protects everyone, to meet her expectations of happiness. Well, that's a lot to put on a new creation! We often fail to realize just how much we're asking our new union to do, and how little time we give it to perform.

Even in the best of situations, love and acceptance and understanding and real closeness between new family members takes a long time. We know that logically, but we're still impatient to get through the tough times and get on to the happily-ever-after times.

We equate any delay or interruption in our timeline to a defeat, but it's not. Slow progress is still progress. It's just the nature of a very slowly developing entity, a stepfamily. It's not a problem until we make it one.

Accepting our limitations

Becoming a stepmom always means giving up some control. There is no way that you can control everything the way you did before this marriage. There is no way that you can impose your will, timing or anything else onto everyone in your home now. But there is much you can do *within* the limitations of your role. You can tolerate your impatience when you temper it with purpose.

> *To everything there is a season,*
> *A time for every purpose under heaven.*
> Ecclesiastes 3:1 {NKJV}

Within your impatience, God will speak to you and teach you what you've missed before. While you are still, you can learn. While you are waiting, you can grow.

Use the time to talk to God in a way you never have before. Let Him help you accept your limitations and work within the bounty of what remains. There is plenty that you can learn about yourself, your family, your God — when you stop fighting the battle to control everyone else and surrender to the pace of your life. It's not a loss or a defeat, but a *strategy* instead.

Beginning your stepfamily is a time to learn who you are again and what your role will be. Stop trying so hard to mold and mend, and instead, let the Lord wrap you in His arms and show you the great purposes He has for you. And let Him prepare you for what is to come. The early days (or years) of a stepfamily can make you feel like you're getting nowhere, but if you use them wisely, you will find amazing benefits.

> *Yet the Lord longs to be gracious to you;*
> *he rises to show you compassion.*
> *For the Lord is a God of justice,*
> *Blessed are all who wait for him!*
> Isaiah 30:18 {NIV}

Pay attention to the purposes before you, and you'll alienate your impatience and put your worries into perspective.

Focus on now

I know that focusing on just today is hard to do, especially when *now* is so troublesome. If you and your stepkids can't get along, it's hard to look at that relationship and be patient for better times. But that's part of learning your role and opening yourself up to what God has in store for you.

If you just wring your hands and wait blindly for improvements, or stomp your foot and curse the facts, nothing good will ever come. Use your time to work on what hurts now by taking one step toward where you want to be. You don't have to seek perfection immediately, but you can honor God's purpose for your time when you use it wisely, when you stop focusing on *deadlines* and start focusing on *lifelines*. You'll be surprised how you benefit from this unselfish choice.

A *lifeline* is an extension of God's power through you, and it has two goals. It helps you meet your purpose for your waiting time, and it helps the situation you're impatient with because it's always a positive action.

In keeping with our original example, if your stepchild is not your favorite person right now and the feeling is mutual, you want to develop a good relationship quickly. But your impatience for that runs headlong into your stepchild's resistance, maybe even your own feelings of insecurity. What do you do? Extend a lifeline.

Maybe it's a truce if your stepchild is old enough to understand the concept of starting over. Or maybe it's an invitation into your life that makes you vulnerable before your stepchild, even if you consider that a risk. Maybe it's a plan to focus on only good qualities of your stepchild while giving yourself permission to accept him as he is.

No matter what the situation is that you're impatient with, a lifeline or two, instead of a deadline, will help. When you say, "I'm working on the relationship with my stepchild, and I can wait for more progress," instead of "We should be the world's most well-adjusted stepmom/stepchild duo by now," you remove your impatience and replace it with purpose. You'll draw a calmer breath and sleep a more peaceful rest when you focus on your progress instead of your impatience. You can bet God's doing the same thing.

Show me Your ways, O Lord; Teach me Your paths.
Lead me in Your truth and teach me,
For You are the God of my salvation;
On You I wait all the day.
Psalm 25:4-5 {NKJV}

Focus on God

The Lord isn't worried about a deadline because His view encompasses everything, past, present and future. He will grant us the same calm if we'll take it. When we focus on His timing, we are far less concerned with our own. When we're working every day on what we *can* control and build and reach and hold, we're too busy to waste time being impatient with what we can't. God's timing will prevail. Our job is to prepare ourselves for it.

When we look at our slowly unfolding lives that way, we can at least appreciate, if not understand, God's control of the clock. When we do everything we can with our own time, especially listening to God, we can overcome our fitful impatience with faithful action.

And the most faithful action is a worship that says God will meet my worries, always, on time, just as I need. We can stop trying to hurry everything along and instead, meet wholly what each day brings, impatient only to learn and grow in our role. If we can do something every day that brings us closer to God and benefits our family in even incremental ways, then we've done enough. And tomorrow will be here soon enough to do it again.

To Think About: Where is your patience wearing thin in your family? How have you squandered time and missed opportunities by being so impatient with yourself and others? How can you give your impatience over to God today and let Him control and guide your work and timing?

To God in Prayer: *Lord, You know my impatient heart. Please help me to go to You first with my frustrations and worries and accept Your timing in my life. Please help me use every moment You've given me to grow closer to You. Help me to cherish our walk and trust You to be right on time in all of my stepmothering work. Amen.*

A Stepmom Prays . . .

Prayer and my relationship with Jesus are vital to my ability to press on despite the obstacles I face as a stepmother. I don't even want to imagine how difficult steplife would be without prayer! I cling to Philippians 4:6-8, and I find so much encouragement in those words. I don't consider any concern of mine too petty to take to the Lord in prayer, and I try to focus not on the hurts and setbacks of steplife, but rather on the joys and triumphs, no matter how seemingly minor.

When I pray for my stepfamily, I thank God for the struggles he's taken our family through, and I thank Him for the love, grace, and mercy He has modeled for us. I pray for wisdom, patience, compassion, and understanding. I pray that God will help me to accept the situations and actions that are out of my control and to release my expectations and assumptions about how and when our stepfamily should blend.

I pray for strength, guidance, and the heart to persevere in the midst of challenges. And I pray for my husband, my stepson and his mother, and our family as a whole so that we can overcome those challenges together, grow closer to one another, and be a witness for Jesus, through whom we can do all things.

I'm grateful that we are blessed and don't have many of the same problems that other stepfamilies have (for example, my husband and I have an amiable relationship with my stepson's mom, and our daughter and her big brother adore each other), but we still struggle with different discipline styles, expectations, and communication skills. Just when I think we're starting to make progress on something, my stepson is gone again, and when he returns, he seems to have forgotten where we left off. Prayer is the most powerful parenting implement in my toolbox though, and the progress that results from prayer is long lasting.

~~ **Shauna**, *stepmom of one, mommy of one*

Struggling

"Behold, I am the Lord, the God of all flesh.
Is there anything too hard for Me?"
Jeremiah 32:27 {NKJV}

Struggling with all the relationships and demands and feelings of her life may be new for a stepmom, but it's something she gets accustomed to quite quickly. It's amazing how challenging it can be to just bring together two people who love each other. It should be easier, but when those two people bring kids and former spouses and troubles of their own to the mix, the test begins.

Many of us (including me) have wondered if our family could survive the most difficult times of transition, from two to one, from yours and mine to ours. We wonder if our prayers will be answered and if we'll truly be able to build something good from so much pain and uncertainty. We wonder how we'll get over the mountain of difficulties in front of us.

And God, forever wise, answers: "One step at a time, with Me." With His guidance and constant attention, we can begin to believe that stepmotherhood is something we can manage, even when we struggle daily, still trying to reconcile such unexpected feelings, when we have more questions than answers.

I know the fear and lack of confidence, the thoughts when you look at everything so hard and don't know what to do first. God says to *believe* first, in Him, in the future, in our ability to make sense of our world. He says to kick through the struggles and learn from them, to be better wives and stepmoms as we tame all that would try to rule us.

He says we can do that because He will do that with us. And He can do anything.

* * * * *

Struggling through Challenges in the Life of a Stepmom

Anger
Resentment
Responsibility
Despair
Envy

A Stepmom's Prayer
for Dealing with Anger

He who is slow to anger is better than the mighty,
And he who rules his spirit than he who takes a city.
Proverbs 16:32 {NKJV}

It's not uncommon to hear a stepmom scream in exasperation, "I've *never* been so angry in all my life!" And there are plenty of reasons to get mad — at your husband, the kids and everybody else in your expanded family. When the anger hits, it can feel like an avalanche on your chest. It's hard to breathe, and as hard as you struggle, you can't move it. It can come quickly, or it can breed over time.

For many stepmoms, confronting one particular kind of anger is a monumental task. They are so mad at their husbands' ex-wives that they can barely function. They are completely consumed by the intense, burning ball of anger that seethes beneath their skin. And they are in pain.

Sometimes, it's the comments she makes or the way she twists the truth. Sometimes, it's the way she neglects the kids or unfairly treats their dad. Sometimes, it's her influence on the kids in a way that interferes with the stepmom building a relationship with them. Sometimes, it's her efforts to sabotage and control the stepmom's life. It all hurts, and escaping the anger seems impossible. But it's not.

Corralling the anger

When we're mad at someone, there's often just as much hurt as there is anger. We may be hurt and

mad because of a direct, personalized attack on us or
because of someone's actions that are unfair and
hurtful to others. We feel pain and disappointment
and frustration and often, the complete inability to
do anything about it. Don't panic — look inward and
let God guide you through the anger.

Take a deep breath and tell yourself that you can
control and manage your anger. Don't be angry with
yourself because you feel angry at the circumstances
in your life. These issues are tough to deal with, and
God understands your feelings. But you'll have to
make a choice about what to do with your anger, and
there are only two options: something positive or
something negative.

A positive approach

If you take the negative route, you're likely to
lash out at those you love the most, say things you
don't mean, and end up with a bigger problem
instead of a solution. You know when your anger
has turned you into a monster before. *Do not be
quickly provoked in your spirit, for anger resides in the
lap of fools* {Ecclesiastes 7:9 NIV}.

A more positive approach is to understand your
anger, being sure that you know why you're mad. I
know it sounds basic, but your anger is sometimes
misplaced or misdirected. For example, you may
think you're mad at your husband's ex-wife because
of changes she made with the kids' schedule, but you
might really be mad at your husband for allowing it.
When you know why you're angry, then you can
make a better choice about what to do about it.

In the example above, discuss your true feelings
with your husband, and be sure that he understands
your reasoning. Maybe together you two can come up

with a plan for the next time a similar situation presents itself. With a combined effort to see the reason for the conflict, you'll be able to get to a solution and not waste your time focusing on your stepkids' mom (whom you can't control anyway).

With a negative approach, you might take your frustration out on the kids, say something you'll regret to their mom, or hurt your heart by harboring your hurt and plotting revenge. None of that has anything to do with making peace with your anger.

The Lord's approach

God's approach is always about resolution. He accepts us when we fail, guides us when we're lost, and shows us how to find what we need when we need it. And He always has an answer for our anger.

It's never about revenge, but *redirection* instead. It's about choosing a positive action for yourself and looking for better uses of your time and talents than retribution.

When you identify and redirect that hostility you feel in a way that works for you, you don't have to suffer anymore. The hurt and the anger are replaced by progress. You make things better by using what you have, and that's always anchored in God's example. The people and events that stir your anger may never change, but the more you work around that anger, the less harassed and victimized you'll feel.

In dealing with that especially challenging anger toward your stepkids' mom, you have to keep in mind that she isn't going away. And as long as her maddening actions continue, you'll have to make a choice. Will you let God show you a positive way to deal with her that starts with *you*, or will you let *her* choices steal your joy? It's your call, and when you claim that power, things change.

The more you seek *resolution*, even if it only means changing your approach, the less angry you'll be about everything around you. And the more likely you'll be to find the answers and peace you seek.

To Think About: How many hours, days, even years, have you lost to unresolved anger? How can you better manage your anger instead of letting it manage you? How can you adopt God's approach and let Him guide you to better choices? What blessings will you find when you replace your anger with action for peace?

To God in Prayer: *Lord, please help me get this anger out of my heart. Help me to see beyond it and to be strong enough to find a positive response in every situation. Steer me away from the words and actions that will only make matters worse. Please stay close and guide me as I seek the solutions that will be best for my family. Amen.*

A Stepmom's Prayer
for Overcoming Resentment

*Be joyful always; pray continually; give thanks
in all circumstances, for this is God's
will for you in Christ Jesus.*
1 Thessalonians 5:16-18 {NIV}

One particularly unsettling emotion that we
often have to deal with is the strong resentment we
can feel almost from day one. It doesn't put us in a
very flattering light, and we know that it's not the
"right" way to feel, but we can't help it. We know it's
not the Christian response, and yet, we're filled with
it to the point of clouding all we think and do.

We have to find a way to deal with the
resentment because it will only destroy us from
inside if we don't. All of the people or situations
we're resenting will still be there, winning, and we'll
be the ones who have lost everything we've tried to
build because we couldn't come to terms with our
new responsibilities.

Stepmoms can resent a lot of things, but we'll
talk about just a few. You may see yourself in all of
these cases, or in none of them. Either way, we all
know that we need a clear and giving heart to have a
happy life. Resentment strangles your heart like a
chicken going to slaughter. God doesn't want you to
feel that way. He can help you find the relief you
need.

Common resentments

Being the mom at your house, whether you're the
custodial or non-custodial stepmom, very often
means taking full or almost full care of the kids. Dad

may abandon their care to you, intentionally or not, simply expecting you to do the daily maintenance because you're the "mom." You may or may not want that kind of responsibility. If you don't, or even if you welcome it but dad doesn't appreciate your efforts, the resentment can grow. You can feel taken advantage of and used, and that's not healthy for you or your family.

Another area of resentment is money. It's not uncommon for a stepmom's family to suffer while dad pays large amounts of money to his kids' mom. Even if the amount is fair and spent wisely by the mom, it's still easy to resent making your family do without, perhaps even supporting your stepkids more than half the time. You don't want to seem petty or selfish, but sometimes it's hard to deny those feelings.

Sometimes, stepmoms resent the disruption to their lives. Nothing is easy, and it can seem like every day requires more compromise, more bending to please someone else. You can feel like you're at the bottom of everyone's list, and you don't know how to correct it. You can feel abused and irritated at the same time. It's not a fertile ground for growth.

Where to start

The resentment you feel is both a practical problem and an emotional problem. Tackle it with an application of practical and emotional responses. Get in touch with your spirit so that you can find the strength to get past this stumbling block in your life.

Start with prayer. You don't have to try to hide your feelings from God. You may have felt like I have at times, ashamed of your resentment and yet unable to uproot it. It can be so strong, and it can grow every day. Go to the Lord with your feelings and ask Him to help you understand them so that you can change them. Ask Him to help you see things from His perspective, not just your wounded view. Even if you think He doesn't understand, He does. Asking for His help is the first step in receiving it. Do that today.

Talk to your husband. It may seem an obvious suggestion, but we're often reluctant to discuss such touchy subjects. You may feel that your resentment will come across to him as dissatisfaction or unhappiness, or that he won't understand at all. It's quite possible that your husband doesn't even realize what you're going through. He may have no grasp of your feelings of resentment, your fatigue, your exasperation at everything your life is handing you. So tell him, gently, carefully. Don't make him guess and don't be afraid to be honest about what's bothering you. You can't build a strong relationship on a foundation of resentment.

Work to make things better at home. As you and your husband discuss these issues, always look for ways to deal with them, and that's what you'll find. When you're specific about what behaviors or circumstances are bothering you, then you can be specific about ways to improve them. Ask for the real changes that you need to help alleviate the resentment. When your days improve, even just a little bit at a time, you will feel the resentment drain away from your heart. Actively involve the kids as well. Let them know that there is a new way of doing things. And then don't be afraid to revisit the issue again if things don't get better and stay better.

Count your blessings. I know it sounds trite, but it's hard to feel resentful and thankful at the same time. Consciously look for positive experiences in every part of your life. Look for ways that others are considerate and thoughtful of you, and cherish those moments. Give thanks for all that your new life has brought you, including the challenges! You'll grow and learn more than you've ever imagined. Spend lots of time talking to God, and in those sacred moments, remember all that you've been given.

Fill your heart what you choose. Reach out to your husband and stepkids and let them become a part of you. The more involved you are with their lives, the more care and compassion you'll feel. The feelings of family and devotion in your heart will help to push out the resentment. You will become stronger and feel more in control of your life, more able to give generously and seek what you need from those around you.

> *So let each one give as he purposes in his heart,*
> *not grudgingly or of necessity;*
> *for God loves a cheerful giver.*
> 2 Corinthians 9:7 {NKJV}

To Think About: What is the biggest source of your resentment? Who do you need to talk to about that today? How can you fill your heart more to help overcome the resentment plaguing it? How will you ask God to help you understand and reconcile your feelings?

To God in Prayer: *Lord, thank You for holding my hand through these difficult times. Please help me to remove these draining feelings from my heart and mind. Help me to find the comfort and solace I need in my family, and please help my husband and stepchildren to understand my feelings. Please help me to overcome my resentment and plant love and patience and compassion in its place. Amen.*

A Stepmom's Prayer
for Managing Responsibility

*And God is able to make all grace abound to you, so that in
all things at all times, having all that you need, you will
abound in every good work.*
2 Corinthians 9:8 {NIV}

Things get busy in a stepfamily real quick, don't
they?! Everything you're responsible for can be a big
load. It's often unexpected and can double or triple
instantly. What if your stepkids come to live with
you, for example, and you go from an every-other-
weekend stepmom to a full-time mom in their lives?
Or what if your financial contributions are needed to
meet child support payments, or you're expected to
drop your plans to accommodate the kids' changing
needs?

Or maybe it's not a dramatic shift in
responsibility that's weighing you down, but just the
everyday demands that stepmotherhood places on
you? It's a time of prayer for all of us when the load
is heavy. And God is there, with an answer.

*Why are you downcast, O my soul? Why so disturbed
within me? Put your hope in God, for I will yet praise
him, my Savior and my God.*
Psalm 42:5 {NIV}

You don't have to carry all of your
responsibilities alone. Just knowing that God will
hold everything on His broad shoulders is enough to
get your focus off the terrifying demands and onto
His unfailing faithfulness. He knows you can't

handle all this life brings without Him, and that's why He's always right beside you.

And when you know He's there, you can forge a real-world plan for managing your responsibilities. You can look at every demand as simply a part of your life you're getting under control. And when you and God are working together on your plan, you can't lose.

Here's a five-step guide to get you going.

1. God is your constant companion, but you are only one flesh and blood person, so you have to set some limits. Don't allow more into your life than you can handle. I know that sounds impossible, especially if you're the stepmom about to become a full-time mom, but what I mean here is not based on the facts of your life, but your *response* to them.

    There are two parts to this step. First, don't start something you can't or don't want to continue. Does that mean you shouldn't ever make a kind gesture or go beyond the call once in a while? No, but you don't have to become everyone's dumping ground or keeper, either. You have to retain control of your time and your sanity, or you won't get through the difficult and onto the delightful.

    Second, if you've already allowed yourself to be obligated against your will, and it's too much, you are the only person who can stop it. Say that over and over to yourself until you believe it. No one is going to save you but *you*. And here's how: it's a matter of holding on and letting go. That's step 2.

2. Identify your priorities. You will find the time and energy and resources for what you love and for what you want. It's that simple. Then the responsibility associated with everything you love and want in your life won't be a burden, but just a part of who you are now. When you know which responsibilities match with your priorities and which ones don't, you can hold on to the ones you want and let go of the others.

   This approach makes sense for you and everybody else in your family, too. When you focus on what you handle best, everyone benefits. And when you stray or allow others to pull you from God's priorities for your life, everyone loses.

   There are different kinds of gifts, but the same Spirit.
   There are different kinds of service, but the same Lord.
   There are different kinds of working, but the same
   God works all of them in all men.
   1 Corinthians 12:4-6 {NIV}

3. Consider the responsibilities you do accept as opportunities to shine! Approach them with God by your side, with a renewed sense of purpose and understanding. Every responsibility, no matter how mundane it is, is a way to interact with and witness for the Lord, as everything is for *"the glory of God"* {1 Corinthians 10:31}.

   Talk to Him during your work every day. If it's overwhelming, ask Him to show you how to handle it better. Maybe there's a skill you can learn that will help you, or maybe there's a way to share the load with someone else. The goal doesn't have to be to rid yourself of all responsibility, but to become more efficient at managing it. Then you are ready for another aspect of meeting your responsibilities: you become a teacher for those around you. That's the next step.

4. Realize that we teach far more by our example than by our language. When we have our priorities in order and we meet the responsibilities associated with them with grace and courage, we show everyone the strength and resolve that comes from God. You don't have to be a superhero or a martyr. You just need to live in your stepmom role, at your pace, achieving your goals, your Lord by your side.

    When you model that practice for everyone in your life, you're meeting one of your most important responsibilities without even realizing it. What a blessing!

5. Even when your intentions are good and your priorities are in order, your role can still be overwhelming any day, any time. Remember through the struggles not to lose heart, not to give up, not to abandon your hope. When your responsibilities get out of hand, go back to step one, reorganize or readjust to accommodate the circumstances, and carry on. But always know deep in your heart that you are strong enough to meet whatever happens.

    It's true that the Lord will not give us more than we can handle. It's also true that He gave us the good sense to know when we're getting in too deeply. Remember that you can't save the world, but can make a significant difference in your little corner of it when you know what matters to you and you meet those responsibilities willingly and with God's blessing. You will find great joy and peace in your journey of the priorities you and God choose for your life. Enjoy everything that comes with them, one day at a time.

Therefore do not worry about tomorrow, for tomorrow will worry about itself. Each day has enough trouble of its own.
Matthew 6:34 {NIV}

To Think About: Who has been setting the priorities in your life? How have you felt overwhelmed by your responsibilities, and what can you do today to manage them better? How can you reframe your responsibilities in God's view and find a renewed strength there?

To God in Prayer: *Lord, I come to You burdened and overwhelmed. Please help me to step back, look into my heart and Yours, and know what matters as I search for the best use of my time and talents. Please help me to meet my responsibilities in a way that reflects You. Please make me strong enough for each day. Amen.*

A Stepmom's Prayer
for Overcoming Despair

*The righteous cry out, and the Lord hears them; he
delivers them from all their troubles. The Lord is
close to the brokenhearted and saves those
who are crushed in spirit.*
Psalm 34:17-18 {NIV}

*It was never supposed to be like this — so very, very
hard!* We've all been there, deep in the underworld of
our own despair. Maybe your husband can't see
what you're going through. Maybe the kids won't
accept you. Maybe their mom is disrupting your life
or overstepping her bounds.

You try and you try, but what keeps coming to
your lips and your heart is only one thought: *"I can't
do this anymore!"*

Have you ever screamed that, or just dared to feel
it? Have you ever been so upset and saddened by
your life's circumstances that you thought you
couldn't go on? Have you ever been afraid that you'd
never survive the role of stepmom? If you've ever
thought that this life is just too hard, too much work,
too much risk, you're not alone.

You're not destined to navigate the strangling
waters by yourself, either. Your despair is
understandable. The Lord's help is near. For right
now, don't worry about doing anything, just listen.

*God is our refuge and strength, A very present help in
trouble. Therefore we will not fear, Though the earth be
removed, And though the mountains be carried into the
midst of the sea; Though its waters roar and be troubled,
Though the mountains shake with its swelling.*
Psalm 46:1-3 {NKJV}

Listen to your heart. I know it will sound crazy, but go ahead and accept the pain that you feel. You can't deal with it until you face it. Sometimes we don't want to feel the desperation and hopelessness. We don't want to admit that we aren't happy or successful. But go ahead and acknowledge everything you feel. You can't change your situation until you're clear about what it is.

Listen to your mind. Sounds a little backward, doesn't it? It makes sense, though. What do you spend your time thinking about? Are you plagued with thoughts of regret or anger, even hatred? Or do you spend your time thinking about the good moments of your life, despite the challenges, and the bright future that will come if you can hold on?

Sometimes, the desperate thoughts are just moments that will pass, not the prevailing nature of your life. Sometimes, they are the only things you can hear. Decide which kind of desperation you're in, and then reach for the person closest to you for help.

Listen to your husband. Maybe he's feeling the same thing, the same worries or fears, or maybe he can explain yours to you. Maybe he can help you see another side of the suffocation you feel. Much of your stepfamily's success is based on your ability to communicate clearly with your husband, to get past your fears and talk openly and honestly.

Ask him to tell you what he hears you saying, and then listen to him. Maybe you've let your worries get out of control. Maybe things aren't as bad as they seem. Or maybe he'll understand exactly what parts of your life are so hard and become the support you need. Don't be afraid to level with him about your desperation. If you hold it in, it will only grow.

Finally, listen to your Lord. Stop trying to solve everything for a moment and just listen. What is He telling you? He's likely trying to comfort and sustain you. He's probably wanting you to stop looking at all the bad and start looking at Him to help you find the good. He's wanting you to succeed, and He's willing to start over at the very beginning with you, if that's what it takes.

> *Be still and know that I am God.*
> Psalm 46:10

When in desperation you're ready to chuck it all, sometimes the beginning is the best place to start. Go back to when you didn't know what your family life would bring. Go back to the time when you were optimistic and positive, when you didn't feel the weight of a thousand hurts on your heart. Then let God carry you through today with an optimistic and positive outlook. Replace one bad thought with one good one. And then rest.

When the despair is heavy, you will be exhausted. You will need to mend and recover before you can fix what's broken. That's okay. Your family isn't going anywhere in a day or a week. Take some time to rest in the Lord's arms and recover your sense of well-being for yourself that has nothing to do with your family.

> *"Come to me, all you who are weary and burdened, and I*
> *will give you rest. Take my yoke upon you and learn*
> *from me, for I am gentle and humble in heart,*
> *and you will find rest for your souls."*
> Matthew 11:28-29 {NIV}

Reacquaint yourself with your personal walk with God, with the peace that He alone gives. Spend some time with Him just listening, not trying to accomplish anything, but only to rest and recover in His warmth and compassion. Give yourself time to repair and rejuvenate your heart. Strengthen yourself with everything He is so that you can give everything you are to your family and your future.

Listen daily

As you work to pull yourself out of the pit you're in, look at each crisis as one isolated event. Don't lump everything together into a "terrible awful mistake of a life," or you will never see the possibility of peace again. You don't have to "heal and be healed" this very second. That pressure and obligation helps lead to the desperation you're feeling. Let go of the panic you feel to fix everything at once. Take care of things, one at a time, with the Lord by your side. Then your despair melts away because it's replaced by His encouragement and companionship.

Just being encouraged instead of enraged about what is to come goes a long way in a stepfamily. Encourage yourself by believing that God will forever hold you close no matter what, and that He'll equip you with everything you need to leave your despair behind so that you can go on to happier times — always in His arms.

To Think About: What one thing can you do today that will encourage you and help alleviate your feelings of despair? If you don't know the answer, go to God in prayer and He will reveal it to you. How will you talk to your husband today so that he sees more of how you feel? What are you

missing by spending so much time with desperate thoughts? How can you change that, starting today?

To God in Prayer: *Lord, please help me with these suffocating feelings of despair. I want to be calm and confident in my role, and I need Your support through the times I don't understand and can't control. Please stay close, heal my broken spirit, encourage me with Your strength, and guide me to a more satisfying and peaceful life. Amen.*

A Stepmom's Prayer
for Overcoming Envy

Search me, O God, and know my heart; test me and know
my anxious thoughts. See if there is any offensive way in
me, and lead me in the way everlasting.
Psalm 139:23-24 {NIV}

When we are feeling envious, we simply cannot
pay attention to what's most important in our lives.
We lose sight of the questions we need to ask
ourselves about how we spend our time and energy,
and our growth as stepmoms stops dead still. Our
future is in danger when we let the habit of envy
color our world. It will never get us where we want to
be.

Envy is a particularly debilitating emotion,
unique and powerful in its ability to hurt you. It
gnaws at your heart and soul because it focuses your
attention away from the blessings you've been given
(material or otherwise) and onto what you see of
someone else's life. That focus is especially
detrimental to a stepmom because she may often find
herself with less than those around her, certainly less
money and fewer possessions.

When the focus is on what we *don't* have instead
of what we *do*, our vision is polluted. With the envy
in our eyes, we won't ever see what wonderful
blessings God has already given us and the ones He
has in store for us. It's a sad way to live.

The source

Why is envy such a problem in a stepmom's life?
The answer probably lies in the many things that she

feels she's lost in her choice to become a stepmom. Because a stepfamily always seems to have to swim against the tide to survive, it's common for a stepmom to long for a simpler, less draining, more comfortable life.

In that vein, one of the easiest things for a stepmom to do is compare her life to that of her husband's ex-wife. If you're living through tight finances and broken plans because of her, it can seem almost natural to hate what can feel like captivity and envy everything your stepkids' mom has at your husband's expense. If you're raising her children (with or without their consent), it's hard not to feel overwhelmed at what should be her responsibility. It's easy to envy her wealth or her freedom, but it hurts only one person — *you*.

The result

All envy comes from not being satisfied with where you are, and it just shows itself by focusing on where *others* are. You waste valuable time and energy when you choose to make someone else's life more important than your own. And when you let what your stepkids' mom has bother you so much that you can't see what you have, you've made your life miserable all by yourself. All of the envy you feel pushes out ten times its weight in peace. The result is decay from within.

> *A heart at peace gives life to the body,*
> *but envy rots the bones.*
> Proverbs 14:30 {NIV}

We need every ounce of strength we can muster to fight this dangerous emotion and get through our other steplife problems. A set of rotting bones to hold us up won't help us very much now, will it?! We can take that verse literally (because we do need our physical strength), but the "rotting bones" of your heart are far more important. The strength that you have in your heart is eroded when you let envy in. Keep the envy out and you can experience a life of peace.

The method

But what do you do to keep the envy away? You change your focus from someone else's life to your own. You change your focus from what you've lost to what you've gained. You change your focus from where you've failed to where you can succeed. Making the changes that you need in your life to create more happiness and satisfaction will leave no room for the envy. There will be far greater joys.

"Do not store up for yourselves treasures on earth, where moth and rust destroy, and where thieves break in and steal. But store up for yourselves treasures in heaven, where moth and rust do not destroy, and where thieves do not break in and steal. For where your treasure is, there your heart will be also."
Matthew 6:19-21 {NIV}

The treasures that will bring you the most happiness aren't the ones you can buy, or the ones that come from someone else's loss. What others do or don't do, have or don't have is irrelevant. It's what happens inside *your* home and *your* heart that matters. If you will be envious for anything, let it be for the closeness and family connectedness that only time will allow. Let your longing for those kinds of treasures propel you to reach them hand in hand with God to guide your way. Those are the blessings just waiting in store for us.

Create and remember special times that you and your husband share. Etch in your heart the connections that you and your stepchild feel, even just the slightest ones. Write about the deepening relationship you have with your Lord, and that comfort alone will replace any misplaced desire for things that can bring you no such comfort. The life that someone else has, even if it's filled with mansions of gold, means nothing to you. It can't hurt you unless you let it. Turn your mind and your heart away from there and toward the life you truly want. Do that with everything.

If we live in the Spirit, let us also walk in the Spirit. Let us not become conceited, provoking one another, envying one another.
Galatians 5:25-26 {NKJV}

Another blessing

A wonderful thing will happen when you keep the envy away from your heart. The beauty of a simpler life will find you, and it's simpler because your mind is not cluttered with the unimportant trappings that envy shoves into your heart. The more you move your focus away from wanting what someone else has, the more happiness you'll find in the bounty of what you have and what you can create. Without envy to guide you, you simply make the choices that benefit you and your walk with God.

But when your life is ruled by envy, disorder prevails because envy is always pushing you somewhere that isn't good for you, pushing you to destroy instead of build. *For where you have envy and selfish ambition, there you find disorder and every evil practice {James 3:16 NIV}.*

That's no way for a stepmom to live. We need lots of order! We need to always find the purest truth, the clearest path, the strongest conviction. We can't do that with an envious heart that scrambles everything around us, causing us to turn our "what's important" list upside down. The simplicity in a life without envy will make everything clear again. The choice is only between what's good for you and your family and what isn't. It's not hard to decide.

To Think About: What situations or thoughts make you particularly envious, and how can you avoid them? What part of being a stepmom can you fill with peace so that envy cannot take hold? Pray for the clarity to see the amazing life that God has in store just for *you*.

To God in Prayer: *Lord, I cannot hide these envious feelings from You, and I am ashamed. Please help me to direct my focus from someone else's life into my own and to understand Your unique purpose for the wife and stepmom I am. Help me to appreciate the treasures of my family and to join with You in creating a life full of the blessings we can only have together. I pray that I will feel Your peace that can banish even the tiniest speck of envy. Please help me see what is truly important in this life You've given me. Amen.*

A Stepmom Prays . . .

Resentment is a strange thing. It doesn't really exist on its own; it is created in the mind of those who feel they are wronged by another's actions. It then becomes a magnet, collecting negative feelings resulting from incidents that are often completely unrelated.

For many years, these feelings of resentment controlled my life. It took a very long time for me to recognize that the negative feelings I was having toward my stepsons had *nothing* to do with them.

One particularly frustrating day, I made the choice to have faith, and I prayed for guidance in dealing with daily drudgery that seemed so insignificant, but was deeply affecting my happiness. I began to face the resentment for what it was. It soon became clear to me that my stepsons leaving their dirty socks in the living room had nothing to do with their mother buying a new car when she claimed she couldn't afford to pay child support.

God answered my prayers and gave me the strength to not only separate these feelings and deal with them individually, but He seems to have also provided me with a new and very important skill: to not utter one single word about mislaid dirty socks. Our house is a much more loving place these days.

~~ **Sue L., Oregon,** *mother of one, stepmother of two*

A Stepmom Prays . . .

I had a hard time trying to overcome being envious of my husband's ex-wife. I constantly compared myself to her and felt discouraged and frustrated. I started praying, and God helped me open my eyes to the wonderful blessings that were in front of me all along. I have a wonderful husband, three loving children and a beautiful house. I finally started appreciating the things that I took for granted.

I still may struggle from time to time, but I try and stay focused and continue to ask for God's hand in helping me.

~~ **Kimberly,** *stepmom of two, mom of one*

Coping

Each one should test his own actions.
Then he can take pride in himself,
without comparing himself to somebody else.
Galatians 6:4 {NIV}

Coping with life for a stepmom is an amazing walk with God. As we turn to Him for help and instruction and learn to model His approach and responses to every situation, we mature in a way that touches everything we do.

As we depend on the Lord to be right beside us, we trust ourselves to trust Him, to let Him be our guide. We know we can't cope with our lives alone, and we learn quickly that only through His love and grace can we weather the storms we can neither predict nor control.

We will probably always struggle through moments of stepmotherhood, but when we allow the Lord to teach us how to act and react in so many ways, we find less struggling and more progress. We find an inner strength to work through our challenges, a strength based on time with and dependence on God.

We find that we cope so much better when we look inward first, when we focus our energies on what we can control, on what we can learn and give, and on how we can stay true to ourselves and build our families at the same time.

The Lord wants a part in our steplives, and when we go to Him with all the confusion and the trauma, we see that He's standing right there, waiting, ready to give us the logic and compassion and ability and discipline and integrity to carry on. *He* is the reason we can cope with the choices we've made, cope with the choices of others, and learn to make better choices from now on.

God loves us so much. It is His pleasure and His work to steer us through everything that's tough. He delights in our learning, our trust and our submission to Him. And we find sanctuary and guidance every time we ask.

* * * * *

Coping with the Life and Times of a Stepmom

Honesty
Courage
Understanding
Forgiveness
Acceptance

A Stepmom's Prayer for Honesty

The Lord is near to all who call upon Him,
To all who call upon Him in truth.
He will fulfill the desire of those who fear Him;
He also will hear their cry and save them.
Psalm 145:18-19 {NKJV}

For many reasons, honesty can be one of the
hardest concepts to find in a stepfamily. Everyone's
feelings are raw and fluid, and the wide range of
emotions can lead to dishonesty. Sometimes, the kids
aren't honest about how they feel or the things they
do. You may find that your husband isn't being
honest about his feelings, or you may be tormented
by lies from your stepkids' mom. All of that kind of
dishonesty can put you under a terrible strain.

Sadly, magically remedying any of the
dishonesty you may be facing is not within your
control. But the honesty that you *can* control is more
important. And it's more than just telling the truth:
it's the way you live your life — as a stepmom, as a
woman, as an example to all those around you and a
testament to your Lord.

If that kind of honesty seems hard to grasp amid
the challenges of your life, don't worry. The Lord has
given you the perfect example and instruction.

"If you abide in My word, you are My disciples indeed.
And you shall know the truth,
and the truth shall make you free."
John 8:31-32 {NKJV}

Abiding

When we abide in the Lord's word, we can't help but understand and reflect Him in an honest way. He will never lie or misrepresent Himself to us, and in that indisputable truth, we know all we need to know. We know about His love and compassion and character. We have the basis we need to become free to be honest in our lives.

With the comfort and joy that comes from a deepening relationship with the Lord, you will feel the pull to honesty in everything you do and say. When we let Him into our broken and complicated lives and bare our true souls, we are free and inspired to live His ways in all of our earthly relationships, even the difficult stepfamily ones. There is no fear.

We can and will find the strength to be honest in every single part of our lives. Sometimes, that's scary for a stepmom, but it doesn't have to be. When things are tough, you can remain honest and enjoy the benefits of that choice. Here's how.

Living Honest

When you abide in the Lord's word, you learn *Who He is*, and you learn that He never changes. When you claim this sweet fact, you can apply it to your life and use Him as a model for everything you do.

Those who know your name will trust in you, for you,
Lord, have never forsaken those who seek you.
Psalm 9:10 {NIV}

Because God is always the same, you don't ever have to doubt Him. That knowledge supports everything else that you think about Him. Let it be the same with you. If you tell your stepkids the truth and apply discipline consistently, even if they won't like it, they will learn to use your honesty as a frame of reference. If you react in the same way every time you have an encounter with their mom, she will learn that you can't be influenced by her antics, because of your strong determination to remain true to yourself and your convictions.

When you rely on God as your example, you can live your life honestly even in the difficult situations. When you make it your goal to reflect the Lord, He will generously supply you with the grace to meet your challenges every day. *Let your conversation be always full of grace, seasoned with salt, so that you may know how to answer everyone* {Colossians 4:6 NIV}.

Just as salt is a compliment to our food, our honest reflection of Christ through our words will compliment our stepmom role. The better and more effectively we communicate with those around us, the easier our job will be. When we live our lives in a way that is honest and sincere and based on God's example, we eliminate a lot of problems just like that, in a snap, regardless of what everyone else around us does.

Honest blessings

When you make the conscious choice to live your life in an honest way, you'll find all kinds of blessings. Let's look at just two.

Building integrity. Everyone has a lot to learn about everyone else in a stepfamily. People without

the benefit of history or blood have to come together
in another way and try to form a family. Suspicions
may run high while everyone assesses the motives of
everyone else, and getting to know one another takes
time. You help that process along when you honestly
present yourself to your family members.

When you tell the truth every time, when your
actions match your words, when you make choices
that are right and pure — when you are honest with
everyone about who you are and what you stand
for — it won't take long for everyone to know you
well. When your integrity is your compass and your
example is God, you are a stepmom with great
strength and power. And once your family
recognizes that integrity in you, it only makes you
stronger.

Moving forward. One of the most unfortunate
by-products of a dishonest life is the inability to
move forward and enjoy all of the wonderful
blessings God has planned for you. If your time and
energy is tied up in trying to cover lies or be
something you're not, you can't be the kind of
stepmom you want to be. Living dishonestly means
living in the past because you can't go forward
without a clear conscious and a clear vision of what
you want out of your stepmom role. And you can
only have a clear conscious and a clear vision when
you make the choice for honesty.

*Instead, speaking the truth in love, we will in all things
grow up into him who is the Head, that is, Christ.*
Ephesians 4:15 {NIV}

Once you've established a habit and a pattern of
honesty, you can base the future on that as well. You

can look forward to exciting plans that are true to who you are and to continued instruction and companionship with God through any trials you face. You can go forward with complete confidence in yourself to handle whatever happens because the truth of *who you are* and *Who God is*, is enough. You are free to pursue your dreams and reach great heights in stepmotherhood when you have only an honest foundation on which to build. There is no other way.

To Think About: Have you been dishonest in the way you've played your stepmom role? What are the hardest parts about living honestly in your stepfamily? How will you begin to build your integrity today? Go to God with your concerns and follow His lead in all situations to come.

To God in Prayer: *Lord, please help me to abide in You, to take Your truth and apply it to my life. Please help me to speak honestly, to behave honestly, and to choose honesty in every opportunity so that I may reflect You in everything I do. Help me to show my character and integrity to my family every day. Guide me in my choices, and remind me constantly that Your truth leads to my truth, and only in a safe haven of honesty can we have the greatest freedom to live a bountiful life. Thank You for Your example. Amen.*

A Stepmom's Prayer for Courage

You, O Lord, keep my lamp burning; my God turns my
darkness into light. With your help I can advance
against a troop; with my God I can scale a wall.
Psalm 18:28-29 {NIV}

Did you have any idea that being a stepmom would require so much courage? It's amazing, isn't it, how brave you have to be to succeed in this role? What else is amazing is how you can always rise to the occasion, how you can always manage to see through the clutter and learn what you need to know and reach the solution you need. Do you know where that courage comes from? There's only one place.

The Lord is kind and merciful, and to us stepmoms who are surely a pitiful bunch at times, He doles out the courage by the bucketfuls. He holds us up when we think we'll fall. He catches us when we do. He shows us the path we should take and then gives us the courage and words and wisdom to pursue it.

When you need it

How can you be sure that the Lord will give you the courage you need? Why wouldn't He? It gives Him no pleasure to see you fearful and lost. When you have to speak your mind about your stepkids' behavior, for example, you'll be able to take a deep breath and say what you need to say. When you attempt to befriend your stepkids' mom, you'll find a way to extend yourself to her. When you need to talk to your husband about your family's problems, you'll be able to because you know that even though ignoring them is easier, it's also detrimental.

When you try time and time again to reach the stepchild who rejects you, when you open your heart to a life that is nothing you ever planned, when you accept a past that colors your present and your future — that's when you're drawing on the unbelievable courage that you have deep inside. That's when God is near.

> *Draw near to God and He will draw near to you.*
> James 4:8 {NKJV}

What it gives you

When you go forward into all of those difficult situations with a courageous heart, you open yourself up to a wealth of blessings untold. You promote an environment of understanding and growth where nothing is stagnant because of fear, and everything good is a possibility. *And let us not grow weary while doing good, for in due season we shall reap if we do not lose heart* {Galatians 6:9 NKJV}.

Stepmothering requires bold thoughts and bold actions. You have to be courageous in your mind and courageous in your heart. You have to be willing to put yourself on the line every day, to expose yourself and to protect yourself. I know that sounds contradictory, but it's not.

Courage in practice

The courage to expose yourself is the courage to be who you are in your family, the courage to face up to your challenges each day by relying on your mind and abilities and talents and compassion for everyone in your home—and to trust that you can supply whatever is needed. You have what you need because God gives it to you. Because He's pouring the courage in as quickly as you need it, you'll never run out. You'll always have the exact amount you need for *your* heart, *your* family.

The courage to protect yourself is the courage to know what you need and then see that you get it, so that you can build the life you want. Everybody in a stepfamily is needy, and it's not uncommon for a stepmom to overlook or minimize what she needs as she tries to take care of everyone else. It takes great courage to ask for what you need and to set boundaries to protect your heart and home, but it's essential.

When you are courageous enough to protect yourself, you become stronger and more capable of protecting your entire family. God wants you to feel safe and secure and protected so that you can easily claim the courage you'll need to meet your challenges. So let Him show you how to protect yourself so that you *can* expose yourself. It works together, and it works because God will never leave you ill equipped for anything you need to do. You can be brave, because He already is.

Do you not know? Have you not heard? The Lord is the everlasting God, the Creator of the ends of the earth. He will not grow tired or weary, and his understanding no one can fathom. He gives strength to the weary and increases the power of the weak.
Isaiah 40:28-29 {NIV}

To Think About: When have you felt that you had no courage, and what made you feel that way? How has stepmotherhood made you question your courage? When do you feel the most courageous? Duplicate those circumstances as much as possible and ask God to help you breathe His courage into every moment of your life. How will you protect and expose yourself today?

To God in Prayer: *Lord, sometimes I think my courage has disappeared, and yet my life calls for me to be brave every moment. Please help me tap into Your courage and go forward strong and capable to all I need to do. Please stay close to me and never let me fear my mission or question Your devotion to me. Amen.*

A Stepmom's Prayer
for Understanding

"Call to Me, and I will answer you, and show you
great and mighty things, which you do not know."
Jeremiah 33:3 {NKJV}

Coping successfully with life as a stepmom takes
more wisdom and understanding than any of us
could have ever imagined. We go through those
stages of shock and disbelief, grief and confusion,
and we make our way to a workable strategy for
dealing with our steplives. Some things we learn
quickly, and others, well, let's just say that the Lord
has to put in a little overtime with our stubborn
hearts!

Understanding ourselves

As we settle into our stepfamilies, we want so
much to understand all the changes and challenges,
lessons and logic of what's happening to us.
Sometimes, if we've come from a background where
things seemed to make sense most of the time,
dealing with a life that often doesn't is tough. We feel
inadequate, defeated, burdened and lost. If we could
just understand everything and everyone, we think
we could manage. But we have to start with
ourselves.

And when we take the time to learn, it's amazing
what the Lord will show us, what He will reveal to
help us through. We begin by looking *inside*. When
we know our motives and dreams, we know what's
most important to us. When we know what stresses
us and pushes us into a black hole of despair, we

know how we need to structure our lives. When we understand ourselves, we can work with everyone else more effectively. When we learn to identify our feelings, then we know how to deal with them.

It's hard to understand all those emotions going around in our heads and hearts, for several reasons. Sometimes, one feeling may be masking something else. And sometimes we don't want to admit and acknowledge the unkind feelings that consume us. Having difficult feelings won't make God move away from us; in fact, He stays close to help us understand them so we can find the happiness and peace we crave.

Peace in your life isn't about burying your head in the sand until someone changes to meet your specifications. It's about understanding everything you can so that you can make changes *yourself* to make things better.

Learning with God

What don't you understand? I know, silly question, but humor me. Keep a record of the feelings and situations that puzzle and frustrate you. Note the circumstances around your times of stress and confusion. Ask God to show you what you don't understand.

> *How much better to get wisdom than gold,*
> *to choose understanding rather than silver!*
> Proverbs 16:16 {NIV}

Put every ounce of effort you have into learning about your steplife through God's eyes. Ask Him what He sees so that you might open your eyes to possibilities you've missed. Give God all your questions. Pray for His answers and watch for everything He will reveal to you. Turn everything over to Him as a classroom, a laboratory, and prepare for His guidance.

You can do this, starting today. The next situation you face that has you scratching your head, do nothing before you go to the Lord with it. Empty your mind of every preconceived notion, and listen for His direction for your first response. Do that, and then listen for the next direction. Learn from Him one command at a time.

Understanding your role

We all have to learn how to be stepmoms. It can take years. We actually never stop learning, and we have to constantly adjust to the many outside factors that influence our lives. But regardless of others' choices, we have to focus on what *we* can do.

The more you understand about your role, the more progress you can make with it. If your stepkids are heavily influenced against you by their mom, for example, learn how to work within the limits you have and to accept that you may have to wait until they are older to build a greater relationship with them. Or if you are the everyday mom to your stepkids, learn how to do that without losing yourself in the process. And if you share your stepkids with their mom, learn how to do so graciously, to understand your place while respecting hers.

Any of these situations, and all the others you face, requires more negotiating and compromise and understanding than a major league contract, but the Lord *will* guide you each step of the way every day.

When you understand where you fit into your family, you know how to maximize yourself. You know how to make things better for yourself and everyone else, too.

Understanding your relationship with your husband

In a stepfamily, there is always the fact of a previous relationship or marriage that can impact your relationship with your husband. You might think that his past wouldn't hurt you or that he would always be able to separate his bad history from this marriage with you today. Not always.

Understanding the life he had before you will help you deal with the problems you have now. Understanding that your husband may have some insecurities of his own, for example, will help you deal with him if he jumps to conclusions or misinterprets your actions. If you can pause and study his motivation before you react in anger, you may avoid some arguments and even help him over his fears.

If you understand his motives or responses — even if you don't agree with them — you have a better frame of reference from which to discuss a delicate topic. Ask God to show you how to talk to your husband about your relationship. Ask Him to show you these possibilities and grant you the compassion to handle the problems more effectively. That's all possible because of *your* growth in understanding.

Understanding difficult situations

The life of a stepmom is filled with the most bizarre situations and unbelievable experiences.

You'll find yourself just shaking your head sometimes, wondering how people can behave the way they do and how you can find yourself in such trying predicaments day after day. The baffling behavior of strange ex-wives or stepkids can make you feel powerless and confused, unsure how to respond.

You may fight the situation, frustrated at the insanity of, for example, an ex-wife who delights in trying to alienate her kids from you. Even if you understand her motives, you're still faced with handling the situation, with understanding what you can do to overcome the assault. You may be able to change her behavior one day, but more importantly, you will learn how to respond to it—by following God's word and by holding on to your integrity.

When we understand that nothing these other people do will change God's control of our lives, we can go on as He would have us go. When we go to Him for our strength and direction, we find the solace and security we need to deal with those who create havoc in our lives. And what does He tell us to do? To "put on His armor" and prepare for any battle that arises.

Therefore put on the full armor of God, so that when the day of evil comes, you may be able to stand your ground, and after you have done everything, to stand.
Ephesians 6:13 {NIV}

When we understand how protected we are with His words of truth, the chaos others cause becomes far less important than we thought it was. It is still real and painful, of course, but our path is through God's footsteps, in holding onto Him through the storm and not wallowing in what hurts. Would He tell us to retaliate, to hurt others as they have hurt us? No, He would use the situations created by others to draw us closer to Him in prayer.

Still learning

We may never understand the choices someone else makes, but we know that the choice God directs us to will never be hard to understand and never cause us more pain. Every moment leads to more understanding when we continually talk with God. Seek to know the little things, and the big things will make more sense, too. Let Him guide you in the right direction when you're faced with an incomprehensible situation, and be true to your spirit that rests in Him.

Know that you don't have to respond to every situation you face with the same anger or vindictiveness directed toward you. You can maintain your standard of behavior even if others are losing theirs. As you seek to understand, you will reap the benefits, but nothing will get any better if you just try to "win." When you respond with poor words or actions that don't reflect God in your life, you'll never get the satisfaction you want or end an argument well. Remember: understanding that patterns God's is always the better choice.

I will bless the Lord who has given me counsel; My heart also instructs me in the night seasons. I have set the Lord always before me; Because He is at my right hand I shall not be moved.
Psalm 16:7-8 {NKJV}

To Think About: Who is the most difficult person in your steplife to understand? How can you apply God's teaching to help you understand yourself and others better? How have you reacted out of pain or anger instead of understanding in the past? What has it cost you, and how will you change that approach?

To God in Prayer: *Lord, I pray for understanding in this very confusing role I live. Please help me to learn from the past, to be more careful in my responses, and to rely on Your control every day. Please help me understand myself so that I can find my way to the peace I need. Please help me understand my life so that I can make it better. Amen.*

A Stepmom's Prayer of Forgiveness

Bear with each other and forgive whatever
grievances you may have against one another.
Forgive as the Lord forgave you.
Colossians 3:13 {NIV}

Forgiveness is an important blessing in our lives, no matter what is going on around us or how impossible our step situations are. It's healing and renewing and freeing, and it eventually touches everything we do. Forgiveness is both a skill learned and a gift received for every stepmom.

Practicing the skill

You learn to forgive with practice, and with a choice. The Lord knows how to forgive us without hesitation, eagerly blotting out our failures when we humbly ask. We, on the other hand, may not have anyone who offends us ask for our forgiveness, humbly or otherwise. It doesn't matter. We can forgive *anyway*, if we want to. The process has two parts that work together toward something far better than a heavy grudge.

1. Separate the person who hurt you from the hurt in your heart. You can choose to forgive the person without forgetting about the pain – the two don't have to come together. If your stepchild is unkind to you, you can forgive him by seeing his behavior as one "thing" and him as a whole person who made a mistake. You need to be able to interact with your stepson, so you forgive him, giving yourself a chance for progress that you

wouldn't have if you didn't move away from the hurt.

Get rid of all bitterness, rage and anger, brawling and slander, along with every form of malice. Be kind and compassionate to one another, forgiving each other, just as in Christ God forgave you.
Ephesians 4:31-32 {NIV}

At the same time, you can work your way through the behavior. You can heal from the pain and allow yourself to put it in the past in time. This experience in regeneration is a remarkable teacher.

Forgiveness is a learned skill that improves with practice, and you'll soon see the benefits. The sooner you forgive the person who hurts you, the sooner you can effectively deal with the action, even if that may take a while because stepfamily hurts go deep. You give yourself the time and space to deal with them when you make the choice to forgive quickly so the healing can begin.

2. The second part of the process is to look at the whole picture, to see the people in your life as the complicated individuals they are. They make poor choices sometimes. So do you. They have forces acting upon them that you may not see. There is usually more to every story than we know. The point is that it's not our place to judge, only to journey.

    When we understand all we can, then tap into our courage, we can be strong enough to forgive those who hurt us, because we *choose* to. We can look at our big, full lives and see where all the pieces, even the ugly and painful ones, fit so that we can build better lives from this day on. Forgiving doesn't erase anything, but it reframes it. Before you forgive, the hurt controls you. Afterward, you control the next step. You're free to accept that person into your life, flaws and all. And most importantly, you regain control of yourself.

Create in me a clean heart, O God, And renew a steadfast spirit within me. Do not cast me away from Your presence, And do not take Your Holy Spirit from me.
Psalm 51:10-11 {NKJV}

Forgiving doesn't make you a victim, but chaining yourself to someone else's mistakes or attacks does. Your life is so much more than a fight with your stepkids' mom or a hateful stepchild. You are bigger than all of that when you forgive so you can repair the damage, when you focus less on their actions and more on your reaction.

No, it won't be quick, most likely, and you'll have days when you'll think forgiveness is impossible. But it comes when you allow it, when you choose to "clean" that hurting spot on your heart and leave the everyday pain and that increasingly heavy grudge behind.

A gift received

So does your forgiveness just give those who hurt you a "free pass" to do it again? No, because people do what they please with or without your blessing. But it gives *you* permission to feel whole again. As long as you hold on to a hurt, you aren't whole, and you know that you can't face any day as a stepmom if you're missing anything! Stepfamily troubles require your complete focus and attention — and a strength that comes from the power of forgiveness. You're doing yourself the biggest favor of all when you forgive.

Finally, you need to *want* to forgive. You need to want to get past the pain more than you want to avenge it, to care more about healing than reliving the past. Just think about the Lord's reaction to us when we need forgiveness. He doesn't have to forgive us, but He does, because He *wants* to. Surely, we can strive to behave the same.

Let the wicked forsake his way, And the unrighteous man
his thoughts; Let him return to the Lord,
And He will have mercy on him; And to our God,
For He will abundantly pardon.
Isaiah 55:7 {NKJV}

To Think About: What is the hardest part for you in learning the skill of forgiveness? Can you mimic God's grace and feel His love in at least one hurt today? Describe the change in your heart. How will granting forgiveness to those who hurt you bring you the gift of healing and hope?

To God in Prayer: *Lord, please help me see the great value in following Your example and forgiving those who hurt me. I want to feel whole and healed and happy again, and I can't when the hurts are haunting me. Please show me how to respond as You would, how to forgive, and how to forge ahead. Amen.*

A Stepmom's Prayer for Acceptance

*For no other foundation can anyone lay than that
which is laid, which is Jesus Christ.*
1 Corinthians 3:11 {NKJV}

As we work through the problems in our
stepfamilies, we realize that we can beat our heads
against the wall over and over and over forever if we
want to. That wall will be there, just because it is. The
other choice is to learn to accept the wall and
everything that goes with it first, and then to work
within ourselves to deal with it more effectively. The
Lord knows when our issues are complicated and
heavy, and He will walk with us to a solution.

Acceptance, not defeat

We can spend a lot of time trying to win, if we
want to. And we'll find nothing but aggravation and
disappointment, because you can't always "win" in
a stepfamily saga, and even when you do sometimes,
the price is too high. But we tend to bristle at the idea
of just accepting whatever is thrown at us and letting
others rule our lives. There is a solution, though,
where we are neither defeated nor damaged.

*Through the Lord's mercies we are not consumed,
Because His compassions fail not. They are new
every morning; Great is Your faithfulness.*
Lamentations 3:22-23 {NKJV}

When we accept the situations for what they are,
then we can begin to work within them with the
power we have. You may not like the way your

husband relates to his ex-wife, but once you accept his choices, you can make your own. Instead of fighting what he's doing (with possibly poor results), you can focus on what *you* will do.

Because you can't control others, you benefit when you use your energy for controlling yourself. Will this approach always get you what you want? No, nothing will, but it will move your agenda to one you can create and change.

Should you still look for compromise and improvement? Absolutely. Accepting a fact doesn't condone it — it just gets you from the complaining stage to the action stage. You start looking for how you'll adapt to the situation, what you'll change, or what you'll do to make things better for yourself, and that leads to a feeling of power and accomplishment. You don't feel victimized or defeated anymore, but a part of the solution instead, even if everything you can do is only about *you*.

> *Teach me to do your will, for you are my God;*
> *may your good Spirit lead me on level ground.*
> Psalm 143:10 {NIV}

What you can't accept

What about the situations that are completely unacceptable? Are there ever any of those? Of course, there are. If you have children of your own and they're being abused, ridiculed or harmed in any way as part of your stepfamily, you can't accept that. If you are being subjected to behavior from your husband, stepkids or their mom that is damaging your physical or mental health, you can't accept that, either. These situations call for radical change.

When Jesus overturned the tables in the temple {John 2:15}, He was calling for radical change. Sometimes, you may have to overturn some tables, too. If so, do it with God at your side, knowing that He will show you what you need to do so that your actions reflect your acceptance of *His* ways into your life first.

Your biggest acceptance

Beyond the specific situations you'll either accept or reject, you'll make perhaps the most important choice in the part your stepkids will play in your life. Will you accept them completely into your home and heart? Often, that answer is determined by them, if they reject you or their dad. But when the choice of acceptance is completely yours, you hold the power of your relationship's future.

You've often read that you don't have to love your stepkids. That's true. You don't even have to like them. But accepting them as a part of your life can come first, and that makes everything easier in these three ways.

1. We love what we claim. Once you claim your stepkids as a part of your life, you allow yourself to look at them differently. No longer are they your husband's kids, but *your family*. No, they won't suddenly be perfect, but neither is the rest of your world. Once you accept the kids as flawed beings — just like the rest of us — you open your heart and feelings of attachment grow.

2. You have an ally. When you accept your stepkids into your life, you have a kinship with

them. It's not by blood, but by choice. And just like that, you're all on the same side. You begin to look for solutions that are best for everyone. The kids are not your competition, but your comrades.

3. Your goals keep pace with your choice. Your goals need to reflect your whole life. When you accept your life as one that includes stepkids forever, you can factor them into your goals. Again, we can deal with anything if we understand it enough and when we choose it. As you work to fully welcome your stepkids into your life and heart, not just on the surface, but completely, you can adapt your goals to that choice. Your goals won't be weaker; they'll just reflect your changing life.

The Lord will fulfill his purpose for me; your love, O Lord endures forever – do not abandon the works of your hands.
Psalm 138:8 {NIV}

Sometimes, we fight the full acceptance of all that's around us, believing that it signals a weak victim who is afraid to stand up for herself. But it's never that if we make the first move. Accept the people you want to love into your life, accept the choices of others, and live your role as stepmom the way you want, the way that glorifies God, the way that helps you build a lasting family.

To Think About: What idea of acceptance have you had in the past? Can you look at acceptance in a new way and start today to live the life you want, by your choice? What does God want you to accept so that you can reach your goals, and what progress can you make today?

To God in Prayer: *Lord, please help me accept all that You have prepared for me. Please help me accept others and their places in my life. Help me hear Your words to direct me in all the choices I have to make, and help me accept my stepmother role as a gift from You. Amen.*

A Stepmom Prays . . .

I've prayed to God on numerous occasions, asking for help when neither my husband nor I would see eye to eye on issues regarding our children. He felt I was harder on his two children than I was with my son, and I felt it was the other way around.

God helped me realize I needed to take a step back and view the situation differently, to look through my husband's eyes and see his point of view. This helped tremendously, and once my husband realized I supported his decisions, he then, too, supported mine.

We may not always see eye to eye on everything, but thanks to God, we've taken a different approach, which has a more positive outcome.

~~ **Kimberly**, *stepmom of two, mom of one*

A Stepmom Prays . . .

I am proud to be a stepmom. I have been in this role for almost three years. I look back on how much I have learned, and as I look forward, I know I will learn so much more!

I think one of the most challenging aspects of being a stepmom is dealing with the kids' mom. Well-meaning friends and family "warned" me about her domineering and inconsiderate personality, and some even said I would naturally have to defer to her lead, as far as the kids were concerned. I listened, I pondered, and I decided to take my own route: to be myself and to be the mom in my house. That is a liberating feeling! Easier said than done, though.

I started out with expectations that I would receive mutual respect from the mom since I, too, cared for and loved our kids. This expectation was dashed one summer day two years ago when the mom provoked me into a nasty verbal altercation. I actually don't feel guilty about anything I said, as I retained as much dignity and composure I could muster during an intensely stressful situation. The thing I regret is our daughter witnessed some of the argument, and I know it affected her view about both of us.

After the bad scene, which left me shaken both mentally and emotionally, I evaluated my own actions and how I should proceed in the future with this difficult person in my life. Since that incident, I have worked hard to remain positive to the kids about their mom at all times. I also refrain from saying negative things about her to my husband, as I don't believe in bringing up unpleasant topics (her!) unless it's necessary.

The kids' mom continues to this day to be difficult and tries her best to interfere in our lives and our household. We've had to change the way we do things now and then to show her we have made healthy boundaries around our family time with the kids and our physical property. Our motto is to remain steady and calm and to do what is best for the kids and everyone involved.

She and I rarely see other. When we do at soccer games or a recital, I say "hello" and sometimes a "how are you?" which has helped me regain confidence and poise in front of her. I won't kid you, though. I still get queasy when I know I have to be in the same room with her.

In the past two years, I have grown tremendously as a person and as a stepmom. When things get out of balance or if the mom inserts herself unnecessarily in my home life, I remember to be myself which allows me confidence that I can handle any situation she throws at me, and I know I am Mom in my house.

~~ **Liza** *from Missouri*

Growing

He looks on the earth, and it trembles;
He touches the hills, and they smoke.
I will sing to the Lord as long as I live;
I will sing praise to my God while I have my being.
May my meditation be sweet to Him;
I will be glad in the Lord.
Psalm 104:32-34 {NKJV}

We begin our steplives in hope and quickly find ourselves deep in prayer as a necessity, unable to do much more. Then as we work through the troubles of our role, we find ourselves deep in prayer as a *habit*, a delicious and wonderful habit that brings God to us every second.

We begin to know Him intimately, especially when He heals the wounds of steplife and shows us how to be the person He wants us to be, not in spite of, but because of our role as stepmom. We begin to realize how much He loves us and wants to be with us, as difficult and imperfect as we are! We get a glimpse of the life and plan He has for us, and we find a reason to hope again, a belief in the future we can build.

All of our growth is not without some growing pains, though. We pay the price, fight the battles, question our sanity and feel like giving up — a lot — but God never does. He stays close and every time we go to Him, He shows us a way around the hurt. We learn to adapt to the change in our world, and we learn how to appreciate all God's given us. We learn how to work in our own hearts *first* to create the life we want.

We grow in our relationship with the Lord, and through that, everything else grows, too. We develop a new way of looking at our whole lives, through the heart and grace of God. We still have growing to do, but we've learned the best way to do anything: holding hands with God, because He always knows where we're going.

* * * * *

Growing Strong as a Stepmom and Daughter of God

Joy
Release
Insight
Perspective
Gratitude

A Stepmom's Prayer of Joy

Be glad in the Lord and rejoice, you righteous;
And shout for joy, all you upright in heart!
Psalm 32:11 {NKJV}

Because stepfamilies that survive are stepfamilies of choice, there has to be a lot of joy seeping out between the edges. And even if the family still reels now and then from steplife fallout, you can still find the joy when it's tied to your growth in Christ.

The joy that decorates your life isn't a fleeting moment of pleasure, but a deep and abiding trust in God and great thankfulness that He's led you this far, over a thousand landmines to the safety of your own security.

A heart of joy

We all know that feeling of joy when a stepchild loves out of choice, when our family is whole and strong, when God is near and we can feel Him. The trick is in holding on to that joy deep in our hearts when chaos reigns above. And it's important that we do, because the result affects everything else.

The good man brings good things out of the good stored
up in his heart . . . For out of the overflow
of his heart his mouth speaks.
Luke 6:45 {NIV}

With your growing relationship and interaction with God, you can speak joy to all those around you because He's filled your heart with an abundance of it. The joy's in the strength of your marriage and the way you've learned to live your stepmom role. It's not perfect, but it's not so far from it all the time, either. It's in your reconciliation of all that's unfair and your victory over all that's hurt you. It's in your deep trust in God because the two of you have been through quite a bit since you signed up for this life challenge!

When the times are especially difficult, we find great solace in our retreats to God and in all that He teaches us. And that closeness makes our hearts a little lighter, because we feel the joy that a walk with God brings, despite the conditions we may have to slosh through now and then. And as we apply that feeling to everything around us, we find more joy awaits.

There is deceit in the hearts of those who plot evil,
but joy for those who promote peace.
Proverbs 12:20 {NIV}

Our focus

When we aren't trying to control or manipulate those around us, but only uphold and encourage instead, the joy in our hearts shows itself, in our voice, in our choice. With the great relationship with God as a pattern, we learn how to seek and find even more joy because we know where to look. We don't let the temporary problems of the day erode the lasting progress we've made, and that fact alone is cause for celebration. We get much better at this practice as we mature as a stepmom.

We can't fight or even try to fix everything all the time, but we can frame everything we need to do in the knowledge of the Lord's love and devotion to us.

If we continue to look there first, we remember Who holds us always, and that is a joy no problem can quiet.

Joy unexpected

When we're in the trenches of tough steplife troubles, we often ask why and how this could be happening to us. We may think of the stepchild who rejects us or belittles us as punishment. But God sees it all as fodder for our growth, a way to a joy that lasts when the pain is gone.

Now no chastening seems to be joyful for the present, but grievous; nevertheless, afterward it yields the peaceable fruit of righteousness to those who have been trained by it.
Hebrews 12:11 {NKJV}

The joy that you never expect to find is one of the greatest. It's the joy of overcoming a loss, of solving a problem, of even being convicted by God to learn something you've neglected to learn so far. Of course, the steplife traumas are exhausting, but they're not bigger than knowing the joy of a God-filled life, or of the satisfaction that comes from becoming a better stepmom as a result of them.

Fortunately, we can bank on the Lord creating joy for us even when we doubt we'll ever see any again! The problems come with a guarantee. If we meet them, they will serve us. We may not know how right away, but they will. And in that knowledge and trust, we find joy. Regardless of the chaos around us or the pain within us, we can rest in the promise of something far better yet to come from the God supporting us.

But the fruit of the Spirit is love, joy, peace, patience,
kindness, goodness, faithfulness,
gentleness and self-control.
Galatians 5:22-23 {NIV}

Joy in the journey

The Lord so delights in bringing joy into our
lives. He smiles with us at the thought of our blessed
hearts and inspired spirits. And that joy is
everywhere we look when our focus is on God for
each step. It's a joy in the journey.

With questions of wonder, we prepare ourselves
for the joy: *What does He want me to see here? What*
blessing might be hidden, just waiting for me to receive it
here? How will I receive this experience into my life and
find the joy within it here?

This approach shows us that real joy isn't a slice
of luck, but a pervasive attitude that creates its own,
always here, no matter what. The joy is a belief in
God's goodness and a trust in His plans even when
we don't always feel the obvious and immediate
effects. It's found in the survival of an encounter with
your stepkids' mom, in your choice for a better
reaction and a search for a solution — perhaps
something you might not have always been able to
achieve.

And when we learn how to find the joy in our
lives this way, we learn so much more. We often
learn how to avoid the absence of it in the first place.
Simple pleasures in a stepmom's life can be quite
limited at first. But as we grow, we learn to latch on
to them whenever we can, and we learn what
impedes them.

Maybe we know that a certain topic with a
stepteen is always trouble, so we choose our times for

talking carefully or learn to temper our comments.
And when a moment of joy presents itself, we drink
that up and resist the urge to make a point or further
a discussion that might kill it and lead to harsh
words. Something as simple as a shared bowl of
cereal without the expectation of anything else can
give us a moment of joy always remembers, a
breather and a smile to help sustain us in the not so
joyous times.

If we allow these moments to come without
conflict, they accumulate and help fill our hearts
with joy to brighten our outlook on everything else.
And when we learn to censor ourselves in those
delicate interactions that can sap all the energy from
our souls, we hold on to the joy even longer. It's all
about paying attention to each opportunity.

The little things *do* matter the most, and they add
up to so much more than we think they ever will.
And the tender Lord provides them for us daily if
we'll only look.

To Think About: Where do you find the
greatest joys in your life? Where do you find joy in
your role as stepmom? How does your growing
relationship with the Lord bring you more joy daily?
What have you learned to avoid so that you have
more joy and less heartache?

To God in Prayer: Lord, thank You for the
joy of being Your child, in knowing that You will
always help and guide me and show me amazing
gifts as I work to become a successful stepmom.
Please help me become aware of Your touch, hear
Your words, and never miss a single joy You want
me to have. Amen.

A Stepmom's Prayer for Release

*Therefore, if anyone is in Christ, he is a new creation;
old things have passed away; behold, all
things have become new.*
2 Corinthians 5:17 {NKJV}

Despite our best efforts, we make lots of mistakes as stepmoms. Even after many years, we still feel twinges of jealousy or react out of fear. And we are generally pretty hard on ourselves when something like that happens, when it feels like we erase all of our progress with a few poor choices.

But God says no. He says that we can have release from everything that hurts and with His help, we grow to understand how.

Release from the past

Sometimes, we feel like the life before this one just won't let go! The old wounds still hurt and influence how we act today. We try to move on, but it's hard. We learn quickly, though, that living in the past won't do anything to help the present, and it can certainly affect the future.

The Lord has a bountiful future for you planned and waiting. All of the time you spend looking back takes away from time you could be going forward. The choice is yours, but God has a preference.

When we choose to release the past and stop letting it dictate our future, then the present gets much clearer. That's because the past, full of aches and disappointments and mistakes, is like a giant mountain we can't see around. If we want to see around it, we have to stop looking at it and look at

God instead. Then reflected back to us is the picture
of a stepmom atop the mountain, still capable and
strong, one who can let go of the past because she
trusts God to hold the future.

And she trusts God to hold *her* — flawed and
needy, still learning and growing every day. When
we allow ourselves to release the past, we release so
much more, and our growth accelerates to heights
unimagined.

*Those who are planted in the house of the Lord Shall
flourish in the courts of our God. They shall still bear fruit
in old age; They shall be fresh and flourishing.*
Psalm 92:13-14 {NKJV}

Releasing more

Along with our own mistakes, we need to release
others from our expectations and dependencies.
When we do that, we then hold on to them not with a
chokehold, but with a warm embrace. We look to
ourselves for answers and to God for guidance, and
from that steady place, we are strong enough to face a
distant stepchild without a crutch of an unhappy
past. Instead, you release him and yourself to pursue
something that will work, to come together when you
can to forge something new, every day, in every
situation.

You are strong enough to love without
demanding love in return, to give without expecting
glory. When you release those you love from an
obligation to perform, you stop looking at their
reactions. You make better choices for *your* actions
based on what matters to you because you are
redeemed and can in great joy *"put on the new self,*

created to be like God in true righteousness and holiness" (Ephesians 4:24 NIV).

Gathering close

The Lord trusts us enough to offer His grace and then wait for us to call Him close. If we'll release everything that we've parked in the way between Him and us, we can bring Him closer. You will hear His wisdom when you start to dwell on a comment your stepkids' mom made five years ago. You will feel His gentle push away from what drives danger into your steplife and toward reconciliation and regeneration instead.

> *It is God who works in you to will and*
> *act according to his good purpose.*
> Philippians 2:13 {NIV}

When we release the past that hurts and the present that hinders, we are free to grow, to explore untapped areas of our stepmotherhood — things we couldn't see before because we weren't looking at God first. When we let the Lord release us from what blocks our view, we have a new view of our value to Him and to our family. We can focus on becoming the stepmom we want to be and let go of everything that gets in our way.

To Think About: What do you need to release today? What can you release others from so that healing can begin? How will you keep the past in the past and focus on the future God has planned for you?

To God in Prayer: *Lord, please help me release everything damaging that I hold so tightly in my heart. I pray for Your wisdom and direction as You hold me close so that I can focus on You and our future. Please help me hold You and my loved ones just as close. Amen.*

A Stepmom's Prayer for Insight

The Lord will guide you always; he will satisfy your needs
in a sun-scorched land and will strengthen your frame.
You will be like a well-watered garden,
like a spring whose waters never fail.
Isaiah 58:11 {NIV}

Few experiences are the education that a
stepfamily is! The discoveries about ourselves, those
around us, and even God occur daily. For a while, we
don't know how to make much of it all, and we're too
stressed to want to in some cases. But eventually, as
the Lord keeps talking to us and we keep working,
we develop a keen insight into the world in which
we live.

Do we have all the answers and explanations for
everything after a few years? Hardly. But we do learn
to build on what we know, sort of like a detective
with many years experience. Along with the comfort
that comes with time, we are intimately aware of the
tiny nuances of our stepmotherhood.

We learn to "read" the situations we face with a
much keener eye. We realize that our starting point
for dealing with an issue becomes about 20 paces
ahead of what it used to be. Our well-deserved
insight is no coincidence. It is one of God's blessings
as we grow, both as His disciple and as a stepmom.

Be very careful, then, how you live – not as unwise but as
wise, making the most of every opportunity.
Ephesians 5:15-16 {NIV}

For example, your run-ins with your stepkids'
mom may have almost destroyed you in the

beginning. You may have reacted without thinking, only in pain and anger. As the Lord works through you, though, you learn to react with your mind instead of your heart first. You learn what works, and you quit beating yourself up with what doesn't. You can size up a threat and form a plan almost instantly. You have learned much because you had to, and it all started with your quest for peace in your life.

Insight and relief

You may be surprised to know this, but your prayer for insight *improves* your insight before God even intervenes, because looking for insight is the first step in reaching it. Here's how.

When we pray for insight into how to make our lives better, we're looking for resolution, not retaliation. We're operating out of grace, not greed. We're acknowledging that there is much we don't know, and we are open to receive. As we go to God with this lack, we find abundance. He demonstrates it all as He teaches us about *Him*. And if we choose to learn and follow, we are forever changed.

We cry for help to work through all the mess before us, and He reminds us that He is in control. We ask for relief from the confusion, and He reminds us where our direction is found. We ask to know what we don't see, and He reminds us that He knows all, and that He will not abandon our hearts as we search for answers.

> *For God is greater than our hearts,*
> *and he knows everything.*
> 1 John 3:20 {NIV}

As we work from a belief in what the Lord tells us in response to our questions, our insight grows as we grow closer to Him. Our trust in Him and confidence that He has hold of everything gives us the ability to see what we missed before. With God in control, we are not afraid to look directly into the many complications of our life and see beyond the obvious.

Every new problem isn't something that scares us to death anymore. As we practice what He preaches to us, we learn to investigate before we scream, to see the whole road before us instead of just the latest bump, to reflect on what we've learned and apply it to today.

Insight tested

Every bit of insight we gain is based on our faith. We grow when we trust that God is in control, that He's directing our paths, that He will show us the "something more" we need to know now. When we face the rebellious stepchild or her vindictive mom, we can approach the situation with God at our side—looking for answers and explanations, knowing how to assess the facts and respond accordingly, because we have learned from the One who is afraid of nothing. *"Who has preceded Me, that I should pay him? Everything under heaven is Mine"* {Job 41:11 NKJV}.

We also finally realize, as much as we wish it weren't so, that there will be situations we can't explain or solve, but our trust in God grants us insight there, too, to see what we *can* do, to spend our energy in the right places. To continually push yourself on a stepchild who resists may be a poor choice. Your insight, which tunes itself more finely

every day, may direct you to write letters about how
you feel and give them to your stepchild when he's
grown. Sometimes, we have to change our approach
and make tough choices, and we learn that we can.
Trusting God and using His teachings as an example
gives you the insight to make those choices, that
*"your heart may be enlightened in order that you may
know the hope to which he has called you"* {Ephesians
1:18 NIV}.

He never abandons us as we work through the
difficult issues we face. He guides us to find the
answers we can use. Our trust in Him grows with
every turn we make to Him, and our insight into
better managing our role grows at the same time. We
see so much more clearly every time we look to God
first, and we know that He sees all.

To Think About: How has your insight into
your role changed over time? If you still feel lost and
confused, how can you apply the Lord's guarantees
to your situation? What one area will you work in
first to gain valuable insight? How will you rely on
your faith to help you?

To God in Prayer: *Lord, please grant me the
ability to look beyond the obvious, to see what others see,
to respond with answers and actions worthy of You. I pray
for insight that shows me more of You and Your plans so
that I may live my life reflective of You. Please show me
the best choices I can make. Amen.*

A Stepmom's Prayer
for Perspective

*For we are God's workmanship, created in
Christ Jesus to do good works, which God
prepared in advance for us to do.
Ephesians 2:10 {NIV}*

Few things in life can make you lose your
perspective more than becoming a stepmom,
wouldn't you agree? Everything becomes a crisis,
and we can easily lose sight of what matters most.
We're so busy treading water that we become
engulfed by every little wave. Then after wasting
precious time in the struggle, we realize that we're
getting no closer to our destination.

The Lord reminds us every now and then to
settle down and adopt *His* perspective for our
stepmom issues — and everything else.

*But those who wait on the Lord Shall renew their strength;
They shall mount up with wings like eagles, They shall
run and not be weary, They shall walk and not faint.
Isaiah 40:31 {NKJV}*

By following the Lord's lead, we are able to do
two things: we can hold out for the good we trust is
yet to come, and we can avoid the depression that
comes with an obsession over the bad.

Looking far ahead

When we practice a long-range perspective, like
God's, we can trust that everything difficult is
temporary, that the poor attitude of a teenager isn't

our fault, that the interference of her mom will come to an end one day.

When we look beyond the troubles of the moment, we gain great inspiration and determination, and even a little patience. And sometimes, just focusing on good times to come gives our heart enough of a rest to get us through the tough times. Our minds are clearer, too, when we focus on the guaranteed peace yet to come as much as we focus on the present difficulty.

> *Finally, brothers, whatever is true, whatever is noble,*
> *whatever is right, whatever is pure, whatever is lovely,*
> *whatever is admirable – if anything is excellent or*
> *praiseworthy – think about such things.*
> *Philippians 4:8 {NIV}*

By looking with that perspective, our minds begin to believe that a solution will be found for every problem, that we only have to flesh out what our heart has already decided: that no obstacle is insurmountable and no difficulty is beyond our strength.

Looking with power

With that positive perspective, you are a stepmom with power. Battles with stepkids are a detour, not the whole journey. Your marriage is the path of your life now, and while it includes a role as stepmom, it is still the anchor for everything else, and when you remember and hold on to that, despite a few storms, you develop an attitude – a *perspective* – of confidence and resolve.

If you're bogged down by every steplife tragedy large and small, you lose ground that's hard to make

up. The grip on a perspective of continual hope and
God's eternal wisdom keeps us going and allows the
joy we desperately need to filter unbidden into our
lives.

*Therefore, my dear brothers, stand firm. Let nothing
move you. Always give yourselves fully to the
work of the Lord, because you know that your
labor in the Lord is not in vain.*
1 Corinthians 15:58 {NIV}

A perspective that looks at tests with great faith
insulates us from the debilitating emotions of anger
and hurt. It's not an attempt to whitewash the issues
you face, but instead, to prevent them from becoming
all you see.

While the disruptive or manipulative stepchild
who refuses to obey you is certainly cause for
concern, a clear perspective will prevent the situation
from destroying you. By seeing the problem as one
issue and not a prediction of the rest of your life, you
can deal with it more effectively. By isolating your
hurt, you keep it in check, segregated and not all-
encompassing. You trust that a solution is coming.
You go to your Lord expecting to find answers, and
He never fails to deliver.

*Let us then approach the throne of grace with confidence,
so that we may receive mercy and find grace
to help us in our time of need.*
Hebrews 4:16 {NIV}

By refusing to allow the challenges to appear
bigger than they are, you can keep everything in its
place, everything in a true perspective. Yes, the ex-
wife who calls too often is annoying, but it doesn't

have to be all you think about unless you allow it to be. With a clear perspective, you can counter every problem with abundant conviction that you will overcome and be stronger because of it. The Lord planned it that way.

To Think About: What is your perspective of your stepfamily? How has it changed over the years? How can you claim the Lord's perspective to improve your outlook on your life? What new perspective will help make your role easier?

To God in Prayer: *Lord, please help me see beyond today, my immediate trouble, to see that You have everything in Your hands, and that nothing will come to pass that You cannot make good. Please help me find the calm and clarity of a clear perspective in every part of my steplife. Amen.*

A Stepmom's Prayer of Gratitude

*But I will sing of Your power; Yes, I will sing aloud of
Your mercy in the morning; For you have been my defense
And refuge in the day of my trouble. To You, O my
Strength, I will sing praises; For God is my defense,
The God of my mercy.*
Psalm 59:16-18 {NKJV}

We learn many things as stepmoms, but
undoubtedly one of the most important is a spirit of
gratitude. When we can give thanks daily, we can
sustain most any hit, because we've planted our
hearts in God's bountiful garden.

Early in our lives as stepmoms, we are often
faced with more reasons to complain than to
compliment. We often deal with many takers and few
givers, and almost no one can understand the depth
of our pain.

And so we cry out to God, and He answers with,
"I'm already here," and instantly, it gives us rest and
hope again. And for that undeniable fact, we are
grateful. It feels good to be thankful to God again.

*You who have done great things; O God, who is like You?
You, who have shown me great and severe troubles,
Shall revive me again, And bring me up again from
the depths of the earth. You shall increase my
greatness, And comfort me on every side.*
Psalm 71:19-21 {NKJV}

And from that beginning again, we find our
gratitude becoming more powerful each day. Because
when we are thankful, we're not hurting. Our focus
has shifted.

"Peace I leave with you, My peace I give to you; not as the world gives do I give to you. Let not your heart be troubled, neither let it be afraid.

John 14:27 {NJKV}

And if indeed the Lord has not abandoned us in our turmoil (even when we think He has), then surely He has sent us other blessings we've neglected to claim as well. As we go, sometimes easily and sometimes with great difficulty through our stepmom role, we learn to see these blessings and draw a quiet strength from them that is truly Heaven sent.

When times are fairly uneventful and crises are at a minimum, you're probably thankful for the respite. The Lord knows when to send us a break! And during the times of quiet, you have a moment to reconnect with God and remember where your spirit belongs, to give thanks for His care and nurture, to get in touch with the One Who holds you close even when you're not paying attention.

Gratitude seems easy, and if it is, that's okay. It's great practice for the times when it doesn't seem so easy. The tough patches of steplife often send us searching for relief, rarely eager to offer gratitude. But when we realize that *they're the same thing*, we find more of those blessings our Lord has waiting.

We ask, He gives

After a few seasons as a stepmom, we learn that when we hurt, we are better instantly when we thank God for His help and guidance *yet to come*, for how He will inspire and comfort us in our troubles, for His grasp on our hearts when our minds are too scattered to think. That gratitude as a first response *is* relief. It prepares us to receive all the love and care and direction our Lord will faithfully supply, guaranteed.

> *"Ask, and it will be given to you; seek, and you will find; knock, and it will be opened to you. For everyone who asks receives, and he who seeks finds, and to him who knocks it will be opened."*
> Matthew 7:7-8 {NJKV}

When we cultivate the habit of a grateful heart, we frame everything differently. When you can't connect with your stepchild, before you despair, thank God for the insights He will send your way, for the resolution He's already prepared. Then allow yourself to receive it.

When we give thanks out of habit for the basics, we realize that we already have what matters most—our ability to love and grow, our power of choice and resourcefulness in a challenging lifestyle, our relationship with God that is both the foundation and the sanctuary for everything that follows.

When we are mindful of God's generosity and compassion, we delight Him. And when our heart is open to receive, there is no end to His care, and we all know how much care a stepmom needs!

When we go to God with a grateful heart, we grant ourselves permission to be happy, despite steplife troubles. What we once viewed as a lack becomes just a fact sandwiched between blessings. With a faith we once thought inadequate, we depend on God to supply what we need, and He never fails.

In abundance

*"Take heed and beware of covetousness, for one's life does
not consist in the abundance of the things he possesses."*
Luke 12:15 {NKJV}

When we move our focus from *things* to
thankfulness, we realize that we're most thankful for
what possesses us – our God, our faith, our integrity,
the Lord's grace that grants us this life to live for
Him. When we live our lives every day for *what
possesses us,* we see that the Lord's abundance fills up
every ounce of our being.

A grateful heart is like a warm blanket. It wraps
you in comfort, keeps away the harmful elements,
and allows you to rest. When we rest in God's
blessings, we find that there are always enough to
cover us completely, to meet the blows to our lives
head-on, and win.

When we give thanks to God for what we have,
what we've accomplished, and joys yet to appear, we
make stepmothering easier, if only because we know
we live this life with the Lord, in His graciousness,
by our side.

To Think About: Can you find plenty of
reasons to be grateful to God, even with the
complications of your stepfamily? How have you
failed to show your gratitude in the past, and how
has that hurt you? How will recognizing your
blessings, now and those to come, make your life
better? What are you most grateful for as a stepmom?

To God in Prayer: *Lord, thank You for being here with me, always, through the difficult and the delightful, the chaos and the calm. Thank You for always bringing the light to my darkness, and for granting me more blessings than I can ever count. Thank You for all the ways You will bless our family in the future. Thank You for everything. Amen.*

A Stepmom Prays . . .

In a few months time once, we had two of our children, one daughter and one son, announce their engagements just three and a half weeks apart. Wow and double wow!

In preparation one day, we went to lunch at a local restaurant with my son (he is my stepson), his fiancée, my daughter (she is my stepdaughter), and Moe's former spouse, her husband, and their two children. This was a first for us. When I arrived, Moe was not there yet. I was there by myself with his former wife and her family. Yikes! My stomach rolled!

I remembered sitting at a rehearsal dinner where four sets of parents were giving each other the "eyes" as they tried to out-do the other with toasts to the bride and groom. At the wedding, things became so stressful and uncomfortable that the bride and groom left the reception (with the *groom* in tears) 45 minutes early without telling their guests good-bye. I didn't want a repeat of this scene at my son's wedding.

So, how did we get through that lunch and many to come?

Prayer. It really works. I prayed for peaceful encounters throughout the entire wedding planning and pre-events. I continued to pray for "the day."

Putting aside our feelings and misgivings, and swallowing our pride. It hurts, but it is worth it.

Making an effort. Sometimes our first step may be small, but before we know it, we are walking full stride. The first step is hard, but just as a baby's first steps turn to a run, we will be running soon, too.

So how did our lunch turn out? We all sat at the same table (Moe finally arrived) calmly, without harsh words, stress or bad vibes. We worked through the details of the rehearsal dinner together. Moe's former spouse and I were smiling, talking, working together, even talking about what color dresses we would wear. As we were walking to our cars, Cricket turned to say good-bye. Her name is no longer "Moe's-former-wife." She didn't seem so bad after all.

I knew my son was going to have a great wedding.

~~ **Paige Becnel**, *mother of two, stepmother of three*, Associate Pastor, Healing Place Church, Author: *"God Breathes on Blended Families"*

A Stepmom's Prayer
for Peace

Now may the Lord of peace himself
give you peace at all times and in every way.
2 Thessalonians 3:16 {NIV}

Perhaps of all a stepmom prays for, the greatest request is for *peace*. A troubled family can threaten even the most centered stepmom's feeling of peace, and a cry for the Lord's care is a daily practice. And He always responds because *the peace of God, which surpasses all understanding, will guard your hearts and minds through Christ Jesus* {Philippians 4:7 NKJV}.

We start to find the peace we need when we recall our lives before stepmotherhood, before we had to adapt to a changing world we can never control. When we look back to who we were before, we see the child of God, untouched by the challenges of raising someone else's children.

And we reclaim her, that child God held closely, and we let Him do it again. We return to Him and start there, trusting Him for the peace only He can give in *any* kind of life. We trust that He will show us how to have the peaceful life we need, and in that trust, we learn something very important.

Even if we get everyone to do what we want, if we turn our stepkids into angels and their mom into a saint, it won't bring the real peace we crave unless *our* center is in God. Peace isn't about everyone doing the right things, but about us going right to God with the things just as they are. Anyone can be peaceful if nothing is wrong. We need to be at peace in the midst of a great many things that may be wrong.

"The Lord bless you and keep you; The Lord make his face shine upon you, And be gracious to you; The Lord lift up His countenance upon you, And give you peace."
Numbers 6:24-26 {NKJV}

Only the Lord can save our spirit so that we can deal with a family where no angels reside. Only He enables us to claim a steady faith that gets us through every crisis still in tact. It is the peace we must have within *ourselves* that stems from that centering on God. It's a promise: *You will keep him in perfect peace, Whose mind is stayed on You, Because he trusts in You* {Isaiah 26:3 NKJV}.

And we can have that peace, regardless of whatever anyone else is doing, despite others' choices and actions. Our peace is not about the absence of error in our lives, but the presence of God in our lives. When we know that we've done our best, that we've responded with integrity and empathy, that we've met others with fairness and respect, then we have the lasting peace that comes from within.

Strangely enough, the trials of steplife will inspire us to that behavior, because we recognize a better life when we see it. And the better life is one of *peace within ourselves* first, granted and guarded by God Almighty.

For I know the thoughts that I think toward you, says the Lord, thoughts of peace and not of evil, to give you a future and a hope. Then you will call upon Me and go and pray to me, and I will listen to you. And you will seek Me and find Me, when you search for Me with all your heart.
Jeremiah 29:11-13 {NKJV}

My prayer for you: I ask the Lord to watch
over you and keep you close, to bring you joy and
grant you an everlasting peace, to comfort you and
make you strong. I thank Him for all the blessings He
will pour upon you, for all the ways He will fill your
heart with joy, for all the steps He will make right
beside you. May you find inspiration and direction
in His words and His presence. May you find
abundant happiness and peace in all you do, dear
Stepmom. Amen.

About Karon

Karon and her husband began their stepparenting journey in September, 1996, bringing themselves, her son and his two together to form a family. They made a lot of mistakes along the way, but by the grace of God, they never lost sight of their goal. Today, their family that came late, their family of "yours" and "mine" is a family of choice and love, and that makes it special.

To cope with the challenges of steplife, Karon prayed and did the only thing she knows how to do. She started writing about life as a stepmom, and she found that she was not alone. There were lots of others out there who knew her struggles, and in that community, she felt a common bond. Karon writes about stepfamily life for several publications, publishes a monthly online newsletter, *"The Stepparenting Journey,"* and provides resources for stepmoms through her site,

Works by Karon {http://karongoodman.com}.

You can write to Karon at
karon@karongoodman.com or
Karon Goodman
P.O. Box 3226
Oxford, Alabama 36203

About Karon

Karon and her husband began their stepparenting journey in September, 1996, bringing themselves, her son and his two together to form a family. They made a lot of mistakes along the way, but by the grace of God, they never lost sight of their goal. Today, their family that came late, their family of "yours" and "mine" is a family of choice and love, and that makes it special.

To cope with the challenges of steplife, Karon prayed and did the only thing she knows how to do. She started writing about life as a stepmom, and she found that she was not alone. There were lots of others out there who knew her struggles, and in that community, she felt a common bond. Karon writes about stepfamily life for several publications, publishes a monthly online newsletter, *"The Stepparenting Journey,"* and provides resources for stepmoms through her site,

Works by Karon {http://karongoodman.com}.

You can write to Karon at karon@karongoodman.com or
Karon Goodman
P.O. Box 3226
Oxford, Alabama 36203